A Human Guide
To
Bankruptcy

LEON BAYER

JEFFREY WISHMAN

Published by Bayer Wishman & Leotta
888 South Figueroa, Suite 1970
Los Angeles, California, 90017
www.BayerWishmanBankruptcyLaw.com

All questions or requests concerning the publication or copyright
of this book should be directed to the publisher by email to
info@bankruptcyblogger.com.

Edited, formatted and cover design by Mark Worcester
Book Consultant: Mark Worcester, DeJureMedia.com

**This book may be considered attorney advertising. Hiring a
lawyer is an important decision which should not be based
solely upon advertisements, web pages, books or other
promotional materials. The information in this book may not
reflect current legal developments and is general in nature. It
should not be construed as legal advice, and it is not a
substitute for obtaining legal advice about a specific question
from an attorney licensed in your state. Bankruptcy is federal
law and your particular state of domicile will impact the
advice you actually receive from an attorney.**

ISBN: 1489580131
ISBN-13: 978-1489580139
Printed in the United States of America.
First Printing, July 2013.
Library of Congress Control Number pending
A Human Guide to Bankruptcy
Bayer, Leon; Wishman, Jeffrey
1. Law 2. Bankruptcy 3. Consumer Rights

PRAISE FOR THE AUTHORS

 Leon Bayer and Jeffrey Wishman get outstanding reviews and testimonials from humans (clients) like the reviews below taken from AVVO.com and other third party websites. AVVO.com is a popular, independent legal Q&A forum where people can ask legal questions of lawyers and post unedited reviews of their lawyers. They (AVVO) provide a rating scale for lawyers based on their own algorithm which takes into account client reviews, peer endorsements, experience and professional conduct.

Both Leon Bayer and Jeffrey Wishman receive the coveted **"Top Attorney - Bankruptcy"** and **"Superb"** ratings on  AVVO.com that come with a rating of **10.0 on a scale of 1-10**. Amazing. This highest of ratings also ranks Leon and Jeffrey as **"Clients' Choice"** award winners for Bankruptcy.

In addition to AVVO.com, other "review websites" provide a forum for lawyer reviews--sites like CitySearch.com and Thumbtack.com to name two. Here is what clients—real humans—say about your authors:

Leon Bayer is GREAT! He's an expert in bankruptcy, is smart & trustworthy. He returns calls/emails quickly. -- L.S., a Chapter 13 client.

I am extremely impressed with the representation I received from Mr. Wishman. He was always professional and promptly responded to my questions, even after business hours. I have referred people to him and will continue to do so. Thanks for your compassion and help and making an emotional experience bearable. --A Chapter 7 client.

The World Class Bankruptcy Attorneys IN L.A. -- mike/kathy, a Chapter 7 client.

I am thankful that I was led to Leon Bayer's bankruptcy website. During my entire bankruptcy procedure he was honest, kind and a true professional. I like that. Mr. Bayer, I am free from debt and my nerves are totally at ease. I don't ever want another credit card. My Debit Card is sufficient. You totally helped me return to my credit worthiness. Thank you for the Letter of Discharge. I will refer any one to you if I hear that they are in financial trouble. I'm glad I found Leon! --A chapter 7 client.

Atty. Wishman is a great attorney and helped us during a very scary time in our life. We went into his office with a lot of stress and anxiety, and he really just put our minds at ease. Even after we paid and our case was filed, every time I had a question (which was quite a few times), we were able to get a hold of him directly. He would be the one to call us back the same day and not some secretary or assistant that didn't really know our case. --A Chapter 7 client.

Leon Bayer and Bayer, Wishman & Leotta are the most compassionate and professional bankruptcy lawyers you will find in the Los Angeles area. One face-to-face meeting and you will know that these are the guys you will trust with your financial mess. Believe me. Don't hire some hack who just says they are bankruptcy lawyers. These guys have been doing this work for over 30 years and they do it right the first time. -- Ken, M.W.

Mr. Jeff Wishman. I am extremely impressed with the representation I received from Mr. Wishman. He was always professional and promptly responded to my questions, even after business hours. I have referred people to him and will continue to do so. Thanks for your compassion and help and making an emotional experience bearable. --FRTAST.

This is the 2nd time that I dealt with this firm throughout the years. The professional manner is so very important when you need legal help. Mr. Bayer's knowledge eased my stress and allowed me to make the best choices for my situation. His assistant and staff are a strong support to him. Well managed office. --Andrea.

WOW!!!. Excellent service! These attorneys really know what they are doing and helped me get rid of my debt the easiest and most painless way possible. They are truly great to work with and I'll refer anyone I know in debt to them with no hesitation! --Michelle T.

Mr. Bayer provided me with sound advice and was willing to work with us through this difficult time. He is both knowledgeable and trustworthy and I would recommend him to anyone in need. --Will

I highly recommend Leon Bayer. My husband and I felt some embarrassment about filing bankruptcy but Leon made us feel comfortable with our decision. He took time with us on our first appointment to answer all the questions we had and tell us about the process. He, along with his excellent staff, helped us all along the way. All the paperwork was handled expertly and whenever we had a question, we either called the office or sent an email, and we always got an answer in a timely way. --A Chapter 7 client

I met with Leon for a complimentary initial consultation. I was impressed with his insight and honesty. He determined that bankruptcy wasn't the direction I should be going at this time. He did, however, offer some advice that might help get me through my current financial situation. If I decide to go forward with bankruptcy at a later time, I wouldn't hesitate to call Leon. --Joan

I will never forget the day I went in for my initial consultation with Leon Bayer. I was terrified at the thought of filing for Bankruptcy and Leon put me at ease. He explained the process and told me we could get started that day. I asked him if there was hope for us and he said "I don't promise hope, I promise results." He delivered on his promise. We were able to establish a plan that is totally feasible. The stress and sleepless nights are gone. I highly recommend Leon Bayer and his firm. They are extremely professional and well known and respected in the Bankruptcy courts. --John.

Dear Jeff--I wanted to say thank you and your staff for handling my bankruptcy. I received the discharge paperwork a couple weeks ago. I also wanted to let you know that the tax liens were released for the Federal Taxes owed; if you recall this was something you could not guarantee, but I am happy to report I rec'd the paperwork from the IRS that notification was sent to the county assessor for release of the liens indicating the requirements for release of lien has been satisfied. I truly appreciate your help and so happy I put my faith in your company! --Kristina.

I recently had my disability account levied by a creditor. I left a message on Mr. Bayer's website with some questions I had regarding my rights. He answered my questions promptly via -email and was accurate and detailed. I had spoken to another BK lawyer earlier in the day and he misinformed me about my options. I was never pressured to make an appointment, just honest help. Thank you Leon Bayer. -- R.W., a Chapter 7 client.

After I spent years juggling heavy debt while raising two children as a single mom, the two years after the crash of '08 finally brought me down. Humiliated and exhausted by my financial state, I sought Mr. Bayer's advice . My only regret is that I did not do this sooner. I had struggled to keep up with heavy, and ever-increasing, interest rates that were far beyond my ability to ever pay back and simply dug myself further and further into a very deep hole. Mr. Bayer was understanding, well-informed, and his firm was completely professional and responsive. I cannot thank him enough. If you are in the predicament I was in, please seek his help sooner rather than later. --Elizabeth.

Jeffrey Wishman made one of the most difficult times of my life much easier to cope with and handle. He and his staff answered all questions clearly and concisely. All phone calls were responded to in a very timely manner; all messages returned. There was never any doubt that my case was being handled in a most competent manner; and I was treated with the utmost respect and consideration. Mr. Wishman will always remain in my thoughts in a most kindly manner. I highly recommend him as an attorney who will put himself out to help in whatever way he can. --JBL.

You are simply the BEST Attorney! CW Thank you to you & your Team @ Bayer, Wishman & Leotta for taking me on this exceptionally emotional journey & being with me every step of the way. It has been a learning process. The decision to file bankruptcy was a difficult & painful one. I had heard outstanding feedback from friends &business associates who went to BWL & had the most positive experience.... -- CW, Orange County, California.

You'll find a lot more reviews and testimonials on our website (www.BayerWishmanBankruptcyLaw.com) and on websites like Thumbtack.com, CitySearch.com and AVVO.com. We would also like to acknowledge the importance of our outstanding staff in maintaining the highest levels of professionalism, work-product and client satisfaction. Many of the wonderful reviews we receive specifically mention this and we are very proud!

PREFACE

 We enjoy what we do at Bayer, Wishman & Leotta because we get to help real people every day with real problems. Our decades of experience allow us to provide immediate solutions to folks—humans just like you and us—based on sound and thoughtful advice. We don't waste time. We get right to the most important problems that our clients face and we guide them through the solutions.

We know that bankruptcy and lawyers may seem scary, especially to folks facing financial stress from lawsuits, garnishments, foreclosures or divorce. So we try hard to put a human face and a human touch on everything we do. In fact, that's how this "Guide" got its name.

For many years we've shared our bankruptcy comments, tips and advice with people through email, letters, face-to-face meetings, our blog, seminars, publications for other lawyers, media interviews and, well, you get the idea. So we thought it was time to put some of our experience in a book for regular folks—even the ones that don't hire us. A Human Guide to Bankruptcy is the result and we are pleased to share it with you. We've included a Glossary of Key Terms and some other Extra Features at the end of the book and we hope that it helps to guide you in your time of need.

Your friends and fellow humans,

Leon Bayer and Jeffrey Wishman
(800) 477-3111

NOTICES & HOW TO FIND US

 Since we're in the business of helping humans with debt problems, you should know that we're a debt relief agency under Federal Bankruptcy Law §526 (of Title 11 of the US Code). We provide legal assistance and help people file for bankruptcy relief under the Bankruptcy Code. The information in this Guide is for educational purposes and not intended as any form of specific legal advice. It may also be considered advertising.

And remember that hiring a lawyer is an extremely important decision which should not be based solely upon advertisements, web pages, brochures, books or other promotional materials. Unless a written retainer agreement has been signed by you and by a member of **Bayer, Wishman & Leotta**, no attorney-client relationship exists. So just give us a call and get things started if you need help: **(800) 477-3111**. Here are some other ways you can contact us or find us:

Our Web Home: **BayerWishmanBankruptcyLaw.com**
Our Highly Ranked Blog: **BankruptcyBlogger.org**
Our YouTube Channel:
YouTube.com/BayerWishman
Our Online Bankruptcy Guide
TheBankruptcyGuide.net

HOW TO USE THIS GUIDE

This book has three "Parts" as well as some great "Extra Features" at the end. We cover all the basic information about bankruptcy in Part I and there are some great tips there. In fact, throughout the book you'll find "Human Tips" (next to the little human with a bull horn) that will really help you. Part II explains Chapter 7 bankruptcy, the relief taken by most people that file for bankruptcy. There, we also explain the MEANS TEST and why some people are not allowed to file bankruptcy after the new bankruptcy law of 2005. And Part III explains how humans can use a Chapter 13 plan to pay back some of their debts and keep some assets they might otherwise lose.

You'll notice that some words appear in all capital letters (like "MEANS TEST" above). Those are "key terms" and they are defined in our Glossary of Key Terms at the back of the book.

In the "Extra Features" section at the back of the book, you'll find some practical information about the Courts and also some key information about bankruptcy "EXEMPTIONS" that may be important to you.

A Human Guide To Bankruptcy

CONTENTS

PART I:
DEBT RELIEF BASICS

1

BEWARE OF THESE COMMON MISTAKES

Bayer, Wishman & Leotta has been in business since 1989. As the founding partners, Leon Bayer and Jeff Wishman have over 65 years combined bankruptcy law experience representing real folks with financial problems in one of the busiest bankruptcy court systems in the United States. It's all we do. And the very best advice we can give you may be in the next few pages!

We've seen tons of heartache and damage in bankruptcy cases where folks made some pretty serious mistakes before they ever filed their cases. We know this because these folks often come to us for help after they make these mistakes. Sometimes it's too late for us to help them. So we'll share our best advice with you right up front because we think it will help you get to know us better.

LEON BAYER & JEFFREY WISHMAN

1.1 Caution: Don't Take Advice From Friends

Beware of misinformation from friends and family.
They don't know what they are talking about. It is very
common for well-meaning friends and family to recommend
that you do things that are actually detrimental. Examples of
BAD ADVICE include: (i.e., please don't do these things)

- That you should remove your name from title to
  or ownership of assets;
- That you should send your creditors "cease and
  desist letters;"
- That you should pay each creditor one dollar per
  month and that means they have to leave you
  alone;
- That you should run up all of your remaining
  credit before you file bankruptcy.

These are mistakes that may complicate or possibly ruin
your chances for bankruptcy relief.

1.2 Caution: Be Careful With Advice From Lawyers

Beware of misinformation from lawyers. It's not just
friends and family that will give you bad advice; lawyers will
too! Here's why. During a recession, lawyers get just as
hungry as everyone else. Many lawyers will gravitate toward
handling bankruptcy cases because they think it's a good way
to make fast money (it really isn't, but we'll explain that

below.)

These lawyers buy a big bankruptcy ad in the Yellow Pages, get an "800" phone number, throw up a website, promise cut rate fees, and *Poof!* They now have an instant bankruptcy practice. Their advertising brings in clients and the hungry lawyer signs them up. Unfortunately, we constantly get calls from prospective clients who have already filed bankruptcy because they hired an inexperienced lawyer. And guess what? Their cases turned into nightmares.

What are some examples of things that go wrong (usually preventable things) for folks that hire an inexperienced lawyer? Well, we've talked to folks that have—

- lost assets that might have been protected;
- failed to discharge taxes that might have been dischargeable;
- had their bankruptcy denied;
- filed under the wrong chapter;
- got the wrong instructions for things they should or should not do before, during and after bankruptcy.

Hiring the discount lawyer is like buying the cheap and unsafe car. You may hope that it will get you to your destination, but you might crash somewhere along the way and become a victim, especially if the road is full of hazards and pitfalls—like the complications and intricacies of bankruptcy law.

Lawyers with the lowest fees will generally have the lowest level of skill and may treat their clients with disregard if not downright contempt. In fact, the client might never even meet the lawyer. In some cases it's typical for the client to have no important communications with an actual lawyer—and instead the client only interacts with office "staff."

 **HUMAN TIP: Check out the lawyer before you hire one!** When it's time for you to speak with a bankruptcy lawyer, find one that is qualified and is a "certified specialist" in the field of bankruptcy law. In California, the State Bar "certifies" lawyers as "specialists" in areas of law including bankruptcy; and both Jeff Wishman and Leon Bayer are certified bankruptcy specialists.

1.3   Practical Suggestions for Hiring a Bankruptcy Lawyer

Here are some other practical suggestions for finding and hiring a bankruptcy lawyer, especially when a friend or associate has recommended someone in particular:

- Do a Google search on the lawyer's name and see what pops up;
- In your search and interview process, ask and consider if the lawyer is a recognized expert in the bankruptcy field? Does the news media seek out the opinions of this lawyer?
- Check a lawyer's record on an objective website like Avvo.com;
- Ask how long the lawyer has been practicing

bankruptcy law specifically. Does the lawyer handle other types of cases? In a large urban area like Los Angeles, quality bankruptcy lawyers devote their entire practice to bankruptcy. You do not want to trust your finances with an inexperienced or part time bankruptcy lawyer.

- If the lawyer is not a "certified specialist," any claims of "expertise" should be ignored.

1.4   A Note to Lawyers Who Think Bankruptcy Law is a Path to Riches

In a phrase, "it is not." Lawyers who have gone into the law because they expect to get rich should focus on other things—accident cases, corporate law and divorce cases. You don't get rich by representing clients who are broke. An expert bankruptcy lawyer with a successful law practice can make a comfortable living, but will not become rich.

Yet the practice of bankruptcy law is extremely satisfying. This is why we do it. There is no other area of law where so much good can be accomplished so rapidly for a client. In most cases we are able to quickly solve problems that have kept our clients sick and sleepless with worry and fear. A good bankruptcy attorney is passionate about helping people

2

BANKRUPTCY BASICS

2.1 Always Get Expert Help

Bankruptcy is too complicated for you to jump into without getting expert help. Many people do try to file on their own without an attorney. However, many of the "do-it-yourselfers" will make serious, costly mistakes that could have been avoided by an experienced bankruptcy law expert.

2.2 The Laws are Very Complicated

The laws and rules governing bankruptcy cases are extremely complex. The purpose of this Guide is to offer you a simplified and basic understanding of consumer bankruptcy laws. Self-help books—and non-lawyers calling themselves paralegals or legal document preparers—are no substitute for having the help of someone with the legal training, experience and analytical ability that only an experienced bankruptcy attorney can bring to your case.

2.3   Consult an Attorney

Any person considering the possibility of bankruptcy relief should first consult with a knowledgeable attorney who specializes in this field. Many people will hurt themselves and make costly legal mistakes by going into a bankruptcy case without an attorney, or by retaining an attorney who is not a specialist - mistakes which an expert may have easily avoided. Often, these mistakes are irreversible and may result in the loss of your property and sometimes even result in the denial of bankruptcy relief.

2.4   How Bankruptcy Works

Bankruptcy begins with the filing of a PETITION in the Federal bankruptcy court, seeking relief under one of the various chapters of the Bankruptcy Code. As you will see, there are other important papers and forms that must be filed at the same time.

The moment the Petition is filed, the bankruptcy law imposes an AUTOMATIC STAY which operates as a restraining order against the creditors. In most cases this stops bill collectors from bothering you, lawsuits, foreclosures, even the IRS. It creates a cooling off period while the court system sorts things out.

When a bankruptcy is successfully completed, the court issues a DISCHARGE. A DISCHARGE is a permanent order from the court enjoining creditors from trying ever again to collect on a debt that has been discharged.

2.5 Don't Get Discouraged

This is a simplified guide and we have tried to keep it that way. Because we are only presenting a basic overview, we have chosen to skip certain complex details that are still important to legal professionals and to the courts. Don't be disappointed if you don't always "get it." Some of the concepts mentioned in this Guide are just too complex to be explained at a basic level. The laws and regulations that govern bankruptcy are extremely complicated. Most judges and lawyers don't understand these laws and rules unless they work on bankruptcy cases every day.

 ***HUMAN TIP: Don't give up!*** Money problems can be depressing and frustrating because it often seems that there is no solution that is just right for your circumstances. This is true for folks even after they talk to a lawyer! But no matter how confusing or frustrating it seems, don't give up! An experienced bankruptcy lawyer will take the time necessary to explain things to you and will help you find solutions!

2.6 Who Files Bankruptcy?

Bankruptcy cases are filed by people who are drowning in debts they can't afford to pay. About 1.4 million bankruptcy cases have been filed on average each year over the last 10 years. In 2012, more than 1.2 million cases were filed; and on average about 1.4 million people filed each year between 2008 and 2012.. If you are thinking about bankruptcy, you are not alone.

Most cases are filed to discharge credit card debts, medical bills and unsecured credit lines or to stop a foreclosure sale or auto repossession. Even income taxes can be discharged under certain circumstances. Most people make financial obligations they are able to afford at the time they incur them. Later on, sometimes years afterwards, unforeseen circumstances can make debt repayment an extreme hardship if not an impossibility.

Many who file bankruptcy find themselves in financial trouble because of a job loss, divorce, or serious illness. The problems in the economy in recent years have also led to extended periods of job losses or reduced income that are unprecedented in our lifetimes. These are some examples of the circumstances that most people could not foresee at the time they made their financial obligations.

2.7   Chapter 7 and Chapter 13 Cases

Bankruptcy cases are filed and heard in the United States Bankruptcy Court. Branches of the court are located in almost all major cities. Under the bankruptcy law, humans like us are referred to as "individuals" or "persons" to distinguish them from corporations or other business types.

Most individuals seek relief under one of the two predominant kinds of bankruptcy cases—called CHAPTER 7 and CHAPTER 13. When appropriate, Chapter 7 bankruptcy allows a person to be legally excused from repaying most types of debts (but there are certain exceptions.)

We describe Chapter 13 a REORGANIZATION. In a Chapter 13 REORGANIZATION, a person pays some or all of his or her debts under a structured payment PLAN carried out under court protection and supervision.

2.8   The "New Bankruptcy Law"

A *"new"* bankruptcy law (called BAPCPA) took effect in 2005. The new law contains many complicated changes that affect individuals filing bankruptcy. For example, there are revised eligibility standards that exclude people from Chapter 7 who might be able to pay back part of their debts.

Those who can pay something toward their debts are usually required to file under Chapter 13 and reorganize. Reorganization requires giving up a part of your future income to pay some or all of what you owe based on what the court decides you should pay. The rules governing how this might affect you and the way courts decide these issues are discussed further on in this Guide.

2.9   Income Eligibility Rules

The eligibility rules for bankruptcy divide all bankruptcy filers into two groups—those who have *above* MEDIAN INCOME and those who have *below the* MEDIAN INCOME. The first group of filers (above the median income) is subjected to a MEANS TEST.

The MEANS TEST was devised to identify--and then

exclude--from Chapter 7 people who may be able to pay back some of their debts. The MEANS TEST uses a calculation that combines a person's real living expenses with certain hypothetical living expenses. It's complicated and confusing, so you will likely need help making the calculations and judging whether you qualify for Chapter 7. But we'll try to explain it briefly here.

Under the MEANS TEST, combined real and hypothetical expenses are subtracted from a person's CURRENT MONTHLY INCOME (the last six months average) to see if there is any PROJECTED DISPOSABLE INCOME left over to pay creditors.

Using this calculation, if there would be any leftover income, the law says that person may have to pay the leftover amount to creditors. If the leftover amount is less than $7,475 over the next 60-months (about $125 per month), then you'll probably qualify for Chapter 7. If the leftover amount is more than $12,475 over the next 60-months, you are presumed "disqualified" for Chapter 7 unless there are special circumstances (see below) that apply to you.

Between the $7,475 leftover amount and the $12,475 leftover amount, there is a gray area that requires your lawyers to make another calculation. We compare this leftover amount to your total unsecured debts (like credit cards and similar general debts) and come up with a percentage. If your leftover amount is less than 25 percent of your unsecured debts, you'll likely be allowed to file Chapter 7. If your leftover amount is more than 25 percent, you'll probably be ineligible to file a Chapter 7.

2.10 IRS Rules are Used to Determine Hypothetical Living Expenses

Under the MEANS TEST (see above), the bankruptcy laws require us to apply HYPOTHETICAL LIVING EXPENSES in cases concerning persons above MEDIAN INCOME. These HYPOTHETICAL LIVING EXPENSES are drawn from what the IRS uses as a *"collection standard."*

The IRS collection standards are used by tax collectors to determine how much money they will take from delinquent tax payers. These collection standards have very little flexibility and the imposition of these standards may result in unfairly penalizing a person who really can't afford to pay any part of their debts.

2.11 The High-Earner Exclusion can be Applied Unfairly

Under the income eligibility rules, a person's CURRENT MONTHLY INCOME is determined hypothetically. Sometimes this causes unfair results.

Under the rules, CURRENT MONTHLY INCOME ("CMI") is defined as the gross income (before taxes) from any source received during the six month period ending in the calendar month prior to bankruptcy filing. This gross amount is divided by six to establish a monthly amount.

For Chapter 7 eligibility purposes, almost any kind of income is included, except Social Security payments and income such as payments to victims of war crimes. For Chapter 13 purposes, income from Social Security, child support, and payments made into most kinds of retirement plans are excluded from the definition of CMI.

The biggest problem with CMI is that it is calculated on someone's *previous income*. The income a person had during the past six months is not accurate in a case where a person no longer has that income. For example, a person may have just lost a job or gone on disability, but he or she might still be excluded from bankruptcy because of the good income earned during the previous six months.

2.12   Exclusion Waiver for "Special Circumstances"

The court has the discretion to waive the income eligibility rule in the case of special circumstances. The law defines special circumstances to mean situations such as a serious medical condition or a call to active duty in the U.S. military.

It remains to be seen if the courts will make rulings that broaden the definition of *special circumstances* to include such common misfortunes as a job loss, death of a spouse, and other serious misfortunes that disrupt or terminate a person's ability to pay debts.

2.13   Bankruptcy Terminology

We've included a *Glossary of Key Terms* at the end of this Guide. But here is a quick summary of some terms you may need to know.

The person who files bankruptcy is called the DEBTOR. A case may be filed by an individual person (that's a human like you or me), or a *Joint Case* can be filed by a married couple.

Every bankruptcy case is *Administered* by someone called the TRUSTEE. A TRUSTEE is appointed by a branch of the *U.S. Department of Justice* to investigate the financial affairs of each person who files bankruptcy. The TRUSTEE has very broad powers to recover PREFERENTIAL TRANSFERS of money and other assets that were made before bankruptcy by an insolvent debtor. These powers also allow a TRUSTEE to recover FRAUDULENT TRANSFERS of assets, to sell NON-EXEMPT ASSETS of the debtor, and even seek the DENIAL OF DISCHARGE or a DISMISSAL of the bankruptcy on the grounds of debtor ABUSE.

Every DEBTOR is required to attend a hearing conducted by the trustee and answer questions *under oath* about their financial affairs. The TRUSTEE can require the debtor to supply copies of the debtor's financial records, such as bank statements, cancelled checks and tax returns in order to help the TRUSTEE to investigate the case.

The TRUSTEE is paid with a portion of the debtor's filing fee, plus additional compensation paid out of assets recovered or sold by the TRUSTEE. The trustee is not a judge. Every bankruptcy case is assigned to a *Bankruptcy Judge* who will make rulings if necessary when any type of controversy arises. *Most bankruptcy cases pass through the legal system without any controversy and will never be reviewed by a judge.*

2.14 Filing Fees and Costs

The court charges a *filing fee* for each bankruptcy *petition*. At present, the filing fee is $306.00 for a Chapter 7 case, and $281.00 for a Chapter 13 case. Filing fees are subject to change, and can be determined from the web site of your local bankruptcy court. The web address of the Los Angeles Bankruptcy Court is http://www.cacb.uscourts.gov/ which always has current information on fees and links to all other Federal Courts.

2.15 Duties of the Debtor

Every person filing bankruptcy is required to submit and sign under *penalty of perjury* a very complex set of financial data called BANKRUPTCY SCHEDULES. These documents include a listing of all debts (even debts you intend to keep paying such as car payments and house payments), all assets of every kind, no matter what it is, no matter where it is, and certain other detailed information about the person's financial affairs.

The debtor is required to provide all of their income records for the prior 60 days. In addition, the debtor must appear and answer questions under oath at an examination conducted by the TRUSTEE, submit a copy of their most recent tax returns (or in a Chapter 13 case, copies of tax returns for the last four years) and submit a schedule identifying all secured consumer debts. This last schedule requires you to state how you propose to treat those secured debts and whether you intend to keep the collateral (such as a car) that secures the debt.

2.16 Differences Between Chapter 7 and Chapter 13

From this Guide, we'd like you to understand the workings of Chapter 13 and Chapter 7. Each Chapter provides very different kinds of bankruptcy relief. Each Chapter has different rules concerning what property you might be allowed to keep and what debts you might be allowed to erase.

To understand why you might select one Chapter over the other, we'll first take a look at Chapter 7, see what it does, and see what happens in a typical Chapter 7 case. Then we will compare it to the relief afforded under Chapter 13.

But before we do that, let's take a quick look at the AUTOMATIC STAY that will benefit all debtors no matter what Chapter is chosen.

3

THE AUTOMATIC STAY

3.1   A Big Stop Sign to Creditors

The AUTOMATIC STAY is probably the most important feature of Chapter 7 Bankruptcy, separate and apart from actually receiving a DISCHARGE of debts. The commencement of a bankruptcy case (filing a PETITION) imposes an immediate and automatic *restraining order* upon all creditors, regardless of the bankruptcy Chapter that is chosen.

The source of this law is *Section 362(a)* of the *Bankruptcy Code*, which sets forth a list of the different types of actions against a debtor which are stopped (*automatically stayed*) by commencement of the bankruptcy case.

The AUTOMATIC STAY stops phone calls from bill collectors, the commencement of lawsuits against the debtor for the collection of money, enforcement of judgments, collection letters, demands for payment and other types of collection actions by creditors.

 *HUMAN TIP: The Stay stops foreclosures and repossessions.* Perhaps even more powerful is the fact that the automatic stay stops *foreclosure and repossession.* So this is an extremely powerful component of the bankruptcy laws and any debtor who is faced with the imminent repossession of a vehicle or the imminent foreclosure of real property will often resort to Chapter 7 if for no other reason than to gain time to try and resolve the debt problem and come up with a method of curing a default.

Bankruptcy is too complicated for you to jump into without getting expert help. Many people do try to file on their own without an attorney. However, many of the "do-it-yourselfers" will make serious, costly mistakes that could have been avoided by an experienced bankruptcy law expert.

PART II:
HOW CHAPTER 7 WORKS

4

THE CHAPTER 7 BANKRUPTCY

4.1 Discharge of Debt

The essence of Chapter 7 relief is the DISCHARGE of debts. Chapter 7 is designed for the debtor who is deeply insolvent and wants to be released from these debts in order to get a "fresh start." Bankruptcy law allows an individual to seek a DISCHARGE *once every eight years*.

Most Chapter 7 debtors today are primarily concerned about burdensome credit card debts. It is not uncommon to see Chapter 7 cases for individuals that have credit card debts exceeding their annual income—sometimes double or even triple what their annual income may happen to be. For such individuals, Chapter 7 holds out the promise of gaining relief from those debts and getting a fresh economic start.

As you will see, a Chapter 7 debtor will be allow to keep (protect) some property, but not all; and the debtor must be honest and open about their property and financial dealings or else there will be bad consequences. Some decisions for Chapter 7 debtors will be difficult but important. These include which secured property to hold on to such as a home or other mortgaged real estate or a car that is necessary for work, but expensive. And there may be some debts that a debtor will not be allowed to DISCHARGE (such as student loans, some taxes, or debts incurred by bad acts.)

5

EXEMPT PROPERTY -- ASSETS PROTECTED

5.1 Asset Protection

Providing the honest debtor with a "fresh Start" (DISCHARGE) is the core principle of bankruptcy law. In order to make the "fresh Start" a reality, the law is very generous about the assets that a person in bankruptcy is allowed to keep. The categories of protected property are called EXEMPTIONS because this property is "exempt" from being taken to pay the creditors. However, the available exemptions do not necessarily cover everything that the debtor might own. Assets that are NON-EXEMPT may be taken by the TRUSTEE and sold to benefit creditors.

Another important note about EXEMPTIONS is that they must be *claimed properly* by you and your lawyer when you file your PETITION. If not, you will face additional problems, costly delays or even the loss of property that may have been exempt. As you will see below, the EXEMPTION rules and requirements are detailed, so you will want to have a lawyer that is very experienced at making the correct EXEMPTION claims on your behalf.

5.2   Asset Transfers Prior to Filing Bankruptcy

People will sometimes transfer assets prior to filing bankruptcy because they think this is how to protect assets from being taken away. This is not asset protection and it will cause harm or complications for you and others involved in the transfers.

This is a good example of a costly legal mistake that people often make, which an expert would easily have avoided. *Do not attempt to omit such assets from the* BANKRUPTCY SCHEDULES. *Do not hide, conceal, transfer, or falsely encumber* NON-EXEMPT *assets.* Doing so carries the risk of being prosecuted for committing bankruptcy crimes. It is likely to result in the denial of a bankruptcy discharge, and the trustee can still recover the property, or its value, from whomever received it.

And it gets worse. If transferred property is recovered by a trustee, the debtor is not allowed to claim it as exempt, even if it could have been properly exempted before the transfer. This means that you would lose the property and you would lose the right to keep some of its value if it would have been exempt.

Surrendering nonexempt assets is a price the debtor pays for the privilege of seeking relief under Chapter 7. If the price is too steep (i.e., you don't want to risk losing the assets), then don't file or else consider filing under Chapter 13. One of the requirements for gaining *confirmation of a Chapter 13 Plan* is that the Plan pays creditors the same value that they would have received from nonexempt assets if the case was administered under Chapter 7.

HUMAN TIP: *Understand which assets are Non-Exempt.* Consult with a bankruptcy specialist before you file to see if any of your assets are NON-EXEMPT. Do not engage in schemes to hide, transfer or conceal assets. Inexperienced people and lawyers can't help but trip over the maze of new rules and regulations.

5.3 Exemptions are Provided Under State Law

The Federal bankruptcy laws allow each state to determine which assets a person is allowed to keep when a bankruptcy case is filed. California is one of the most generous of all states when it comes to exemptions. The state exemptions are set forth in two separate lists, which are found in California Code of Civil Procedure (CCP) §703 and §704. (See "Extra Features" at the end of the book and the Section titled "Current Dollar Amounts of California Exemptions From Enforcement of Judgment".)

5.4 California has Two Different Sets of Exemptions

The debtor is allowed to use the exemptions from only one "list" or "set" of exemptions. These are either California Code of Civil Procedure (CCP) §703 or §704. We cannot "mix and match" from the two. There are some similarities between these exemption lists, but also some major differences. Therefore, expert legal guidance is imperative for any person filing bankruptcy. The failure to correctly plan for the bankruptcy filing and use the correct exemptions can actually cause some people to lose property that they could have protected.

5.5 Successful Exemption Planning

Proper exemption planning is essential to successfully accomplishing the Debtor's goal of protecting assets. However, great care must be taken. Non-attorneys, such as the so-called legal document preparers, paralegals or other non-attorneys, cannot be relied upon to properly guide a person through the legal maze of bankruptcy laws, especially when doing appropriate exemption planning.

HUMAN TIP: Don't mix and match exemptions from California's two separate exemption lists. You cannot "mix and match" by combining exemptions from one list with any of the exemptions on the other list. Always check with an expert before taking any legal action, as the laws sometimes change, and court rulings will occasionally affect the manner in which these laws are applied and interpreted.

5.6   Risk of Losing Assets

Exemptions may protect property up to certain dollar limits. If the property has more equity in it than can be covered by every applicable exemption (sometimes an asset may be cross-covered covered by more than one exemption), the bankruptcy trustee may sell the property.

When the trustee sells the asset, the trustee will pay the amount of the exemption to the debtor and retain the NON-EXEMPT amount of equity for the bankruptcy estate. Money kept by the bankruptcy estate is used to pay the expenses of bankruptcy administration, and the remainder is distributed to creditors.

5.7   Priority Claims Get Paid Ahead of Other Creditors From Non Exempt Property

Money that is available in an estate to pay creditors is distributed according to a *pro rata* method of *priority*. Certain claims have priority and are paid first before other creditors receive anything. These priority claims include unpaid family support and most types of tax claims. They will be paid before *non-priority unsecured claims* such as credit card debts. If there is not enough money to pay all the allowed claims in full, you would see a situation where priority claims may receive a distribution and leave no money to pay anything to non-priority unsecured claims. For example, delinquent tax claims and the bankruptcy trustee might get paid from recovered assets, but general creditors (claims from credit cards, medical bills, etc.) might get nothing.

5.8 Where to Find the List of Exemptions

Below is a website url where you can find the exemptions that are available to debtors who file a bankruptcy case in *California*. You'll also find these lists of California EXEMPTIONS at the end of this book. The *California* debtors can choose between the two separate sets of exemptions. Depending on the kind of assets that the debtor owns, one set of exemptions may be much more favorable to a particular debtor than what is available under the other set.

Exemption planning is an art and the exemption planning is best performed under the guidance of an experienced bankruptcy attorney. The two lists of California exemptions can be found at the following website:

http://www.courts.ca.gov/documents/ej156.pdf

Please note that these government websites change from time to time; and the above link is active as of May 2013.

 ***HUMAN TIP:*** *Sometimes your state of residence before bankruptcy will affect exemptions you get to use.* Special exemption rules are a good example of why you need expert help. The bankruptcy law also places certain exclusions on property that can be claimed as exempt where the debtor has not been domiciled (residing) in the same state for at least 730 days before the filing of the bankruptcy case. Under these exclusions, the debtor may be required to use the exemptions of the state where the debtor used to live, instead of the state where the debtor now lives.

6

BANKRUPTCY ABUSE -- YOUR CASE MAY BE DISMISSED ON THE GROUNDS OF "ABUSE"

6.1   Traditional Basis for Finding Abuse

A chapter 7 case filed by a person with primarily CONSUMER DEBTS may be dismissed (or converted to a Chapter 13 case if the debtor agrees) where the court finds that the granting of relief under chapter 7 would be an abuse of the law.

The standard that courts use to decide this (abuse) is whether the debtor can afford to pay back a significant amount of his or her debts over time. So courts will examine the debtor's ability to pay all or a substantial portion of debt (i.e., in a Chapter 13 case) over a reasonable period of time as an alternative to Chapter 7.

Courts will consider the likely result of a hypothetical

Chapter 13 case for the debtor in order to decide whether an abuse of Chapter 7 is likely to occur. However, the "new" bankruptcy law of 2005 has added a whole new dimension to this process. The amended law provides that in certain instances, *the court will presume that abuse exits* where the debtor is subject to and fails what has become known as a MEANS TEST.

6.2 "Presumption of Abuse" and the "Means Test"

The *new bankruptcy law of* 2005 established a mechanical test or formula for deciding when this "presumption of abuse" exists in a Chapter 7 filing. The actual rules are extremely complex and can be found in Bankruptcy Code §707(b). The following description is something of an over simplification but will help you to understand the main elements of the MEANS TEST and how it operates:

Income tables establish the MEDIAN INCOME **for your case.** First, all debtors are divided into two categories: Those with annual income above the MEDIAN INCOME level for a similar household in the same state, and those with below the MEDIAN INCOME level for a similar household in the same state where the debtor resides. To see the actual tables for these income levels, go to the United States Department of Justice website and the key pages: www.justice.gov/ust/eo/bapcpa/20110315/bci_data/median _income_table.htm.

BELOW MEDIAN INCOME. Debtors who have below this MEDIAN INCOME in their state/area are subject to an abuse dismissal standard similar to what has been used traditionally (see above). That is, the court will examine the debtor's income and living expenses to see if the debtor could actually afford to pay all or a substantial portion of their debt over a reasonable period of time. In addition, the court shall consider if the bankruptcy case was filed in *"bad faith"* and also consider if the "totality of the circumstances of the debtor's financial situation demonstrates abuse."

ABOVE MEDIAN INCOME. Debtors who have income above the MEDIAN INCOME level for their state/area are subjected to a MEANS TEST that is a formula. It is partly based on actual living expenses and partially based on hypothetical living expenses. As a result, it can be arbitrary and unfair. But if the MEANS TEST is applied to you and you don't "pass," then you are guilty of PRESUMED ABUSE. Without special circumstances, you won't be allowed to file Chapter 7. We describe how it works below.

HUMAN TIP: "Abuse" sounds bad, but it's good to be earning money, so talk to a lawyer quick! We are very pleased when our clients are earning good money, especially after periods of extended unemployment or similar problems. If you are above the median income, don't take chances with the rules explained below—see a qualified attorney right away! If this is your situation, don't fret about it. Talk to us as soon as possible so that we may help you understand how the rules affect you. And remember, the rules look at your income in the last 6 months, so you should talk to a lawyer as soon as possible to see how the rules will affect your case.

6.3   How the Means Test Works

We start with your CURRENT MONTHLY INCOME
(explained below). Then we subtract a combination of *real*
and *hypothetical* living expenses. This is supposed to tell
you and your attorneys if you have enough PROJECTED
DISPOSABLE INCOME to pay some of your debts.

Presumption of abuse is automatic for debtors with
above MEDIAN INCOME if they have enough
PROJECTED DISPOSABLE INCOME to pay general
unsecured creditors:

- At least $12,475 over a period of 60 months;
- At least 25% of these general unsecured debts if the
  projected disposable income totals between $7,475
  and $12,475 over a period of 60 months;
- And if the PROJECTED DISPOSABLE INCOME
  is not enough to pay at least $7,475 over a 60 month
  period, there is **no** *presumption of abuse* –
  However, the debtor may be subject to the other
  provisions allowing dismissal if the bankruptcy case
  was filed in *"bad faith"* and also considering if the
  "totality of the circumstances of the debtor's
  financial situation demonstrates abuse."

CURRENT MONTHLY INCOME under the MEANS
TEST refers to all of the debtor's income received during the
last six calendar months ending with the month prior to
the bankruptcy filing. But note that Social Security and

income of the debtor's spouse (if it is not shared with the debtor) are excluded from the definition of current monthly income. The PROJECTED DISPOSABLE INCOME is what the debtor has left over after subtracting the required combination of real and hypothetical living expenses from the debtor's CURRENT MONTHLY INCOME (see below).

The MEANS TEST employs a combination of real and hypothetical living expenses to determine ability to pay. If ability to pay is found, then the bankruptcy case is **presumed to be an abuse.** The hypothetical expenses are taken from the expense standards that are used by the IRS to determine the size of monthly payments that it will collect from delinquent tax payers. To see this in detail, go to the U.S. Department of Justice website (see Other Bankruptcy Resources at the back of this book) where you will find the national and local expense standards that will apply to you.

HUMAN TIP: "Special Circumstances" (discussed below) may change over time as courts make more rulings. Over time the courts will probably issue many rulings that define the term "special circumstances" that would allow you to file Chapter 7 even if you fail the MEANS TEST. A sudden job loss or other major income disruption—such as one that comes from a serious disease or disability—will probably be sufficient to establish inability to pay (see more below). Of course, the debtor would still have to show convincing evidence that the disruption to income or the extra expense is likely to persist for the foreseeable future and was not created as a bad faith tactic (such as deliberately quitting a job).

6.4 Special Circumstances may be Used to Get Relief from the Means Test

A presumption of abuse finding may be overcome by demonstrating "special circumstances." **Special circumstances** is defined in the law as "a serious medical condition or a call to active duty in the Armed Forces, to the extent such special circumstances that justify additional expenses or adjustments of current monthly income for which there is no reasonable alternative." In order to establish special circumstances the debtor must provide documentation and a detailed explanation that makes the claimed extra expenses or adjustment of income necessary and reasonable.

 *HUMAN TIP: But the net income portion of the means test may still apply.* Of course, to get the benefit of the "special circumstances" exception, you'd still have to show that you won't have enough left over income going forward under the MEANS TEST despite your circumstances. So the additional expenses or adjustments to income claimed by the debtor under this section must establish that the debtor's projected disposable income does not leave enough money to pay the general creditors at least $12,475 over a period of 60 months or at least 25% of such debts if the projected disposable income is between $7,475 and $12,475. If the projected disposable income is less than $7,475 over the next 60 months, the presumption of abuse will be rebutted.

6.5   Attorneys Beware

We often get calls from debtors that want us to take over their cases when the first attorney is in trouble with the bankruptcy court or has made mistakes in the case. This is unfortunate and it is the reason that we so strongly advise people to use an experienced bankruptcy attorney, preferably one that is also a CERTIFIED BANKRUPTCY SPECIALIST.

We sometimes get these same calls from the lawyers that are in trouble. So we'll take this opportunity here to caution the lawyers directly about the dangers of representing debtors without a clear understanding of the consequences and without solid procedures in place in their office that are designed to prevent or discover problems in their filings.

There is **attorney liability** as well as possible **sanctions** against lawyers for filing a case that the court finds is an *abuse* of Chapter 7! Because this subsection is really intended for lawyers to read, we have reproduced below the actual text of the relevant statute, found in the new *Bankruptcy Code* at *Section 707(4)(A)*:

(4)(A) The court, on its own initiative or on the motion of a party in interest, in accordance with the procedures described in rule 9011 of the Federal Rules of Bankruptcy Procedure, may order the attorney for the debtor to reimburse the trustee for all reasonable costs in prosecuting a motion filed under section 707(b), including reasonable attorneys' fees, if-

(i) a trustee files a motion for dismissal or conversion under this subsection; and

(ii) the court--

(I) grants such motion; and (II) finds that the action of

the attorney for the debtor in filing a case under this chapter violated rule 9011 of the Federal Rules of Bankruptcy Procedure.

(B) If the court finds that the attorney for the debtor violated rule 9011 of the Federal Rules of Bankruptcy Procedure, the court, on its own initiative or on the motion of a party in interest, in accordance with such procedures, may order--

(i) the assessment of an appropriate civil penalty against the attorney for the debtor; and (ii) the payment of such civil penalty to the trustee, the United States trustee (or the bankruptcy administrator, if any).

(C) The signature of an attorney on a petition, pleading, or written motion shall constitute a certification that the attorney has--

(i) performed a reasonable investigation into the circumstances that gave rise to the petition, pleading, or written motion; and (ii) determined that the petition, pleading, or written motion--

(I) is well grounded in fact; and

(II) is warranted by existing law or a good faith argument for the extension, modification, or reversal of existing law and does not constitute an abuse under paragraph (1).

(D) The signature of an attorney on the petition shall constitute a certification that the attorney has no knowledge after an inquiry that the information in the schedules filed with such petition is incorrect.

7

CHAPTER 7 EFFECT ON LIENS

7.1   Liens Normally Remain

One of the most fundamental protections for creditors under Chapter 7 is the fact that liens normally pass through Chapter 7 unaffected by the debtor's discharge. This means that if a creditor has a lien or a mortgage on your property, and if there is no way to "avoid" the lien (see below), then the creditor will be allowed to take back the collateral at some point after you file bankruptcy if you don't make payments and honor the original contract terms.

7.2   Types of Liens

A lien is a security interest affecting some type of property owned by the debtor. Most typically in a bankruptcy case it is going to be a lien or a mortgage secured by the debtor's residence or other real property, or the title slip to a motor vehicle that has money owed on it.

Purchase money security interests in appliances and furniture are also common examples of assets that may be subject to a lien. Basically, a "lien" is usually found on something that the debtor purchased and for which the debtor has not finished paying. When the debtor files bankruptcy, the debtor can usually keep such an asset provided that the debtor continues to pay for the item and honor the original contract.

Other liens that do not come about when the debtor purchases an item are called "non-purchase money" liens. Recently short term loans on autos (so-called "title loans") have grown in popularity and this would be a type of non-purchase money loan. Or if a creditor got a judgment against you before bankruptcy, they may have taken steps to "lien" your property with that judgment. This is also considered a non-purchase money lien.

7.3   Avoiding Liens

Some liens are *avoidable* (removable) by the debtor. But when a lien is avoidable, a special action must be taken in the court. **It does not happen automatically.** And when the correct actions are filed in court, it is the debtor's burden to **prove with facts** that each of the required circumstances exist that legally permit the court to order the avoidance of the lien (or at least part of the lien).

Generally, liens can be avoided against assets, but only up to the amount of any exemption that the debtor was entitled to claim on the affected asset; and provided that the lien arose as a judgment lien, or as a *nonpossessory, nonpurchase money lien* on certain kinds of household goods and personal effects belonging to the debtor. The terms *"non-possessory, non-purchase money"* mean that the debtor already owned the asset before it was ever pledged as collateral for the debt, and the creditor did not keep possession of the asset as security for the debt.

 ***HUMAN TIP:*** Here are some examples of liens and what actually happens to humans in Chapter 7:

- **Jewelry held in pawn.** It is not subject to lien avoidance. You lose it because a pawnbroker keeps possession of the jewelry until the loan is paid in full. For this reason, the loan isn't "non-possessory." In case you are trying to follow this as a human, "possession" is the opposite of "non-possessory."

- **You put up your home furnishings as collateral for a loan.** A debtor who has borrowed money from a loan company by using home furniture and appliances as collateral for the loan can usually avoid the lien. You may win. This is because such furniture and appliances are usually EXEMPT, the debtor did not use the borrowed money to buy those assets, and the debtor did not have to surrender possession of the collateral until the loan was repaid. As you can see, in this case the necessary elements of a non-possessory, non-purchase money lien against EXEMPT property have been met.

- **A judgment lien was recorded against your house.** These are usually avoidable IF the equity in your home that the lien took away would have been protected as EXEMPT (e.g., by the California homestead exemption). We look at your property as if the judgment lien wasn't there. If there is equity over your valid mortgage(s), and if that equity would have been EXEMPT, you probably will get to erase the judgment lien if you take the proper steps in court and prove the necessary facts. Of course, you'll still have to pay your mortgage(s) if you want to keep your house.

7.4 Statutory Liens are not Avoidable by the Debtor

There are certain liens called *statutory liens* that the debtor cannot avoid. Examples are tax liens and mechanic's liens.

 *HUMAN TIP: Remember, you have to take special actions in court to avoid (remove) a lien.* Certain liens against exempt property are avoidable by the debtor, but the lien avoidance does not happen automatically. The debtor must take affirmative legal action in court to get a separate court order avoiding the lien. Unless the debtor takes these steps, the lien remains against the debtor's property and can still be enforced by the creditor, after the case is closed. This is true even though that lien could have been avoided during the case.

8

REOPENING A CLOSED CASE

The court will usually permit the debtor to *reopen* a case so that the debtor can seek relief that could have been sought (but perhaps was overlooked) during the bankruptcy. For example, during the bankruptcy case the debtor might not have been aware of a judgment lien and only learned about the lien years later. In that case the debtor might seek to reopen the closed case in order to then file a motion seeking to avoid the lien.

9

REAFFIRMATION OF DEBTS, REDEMPTION OF COLLATERAL (YOUR PROPERTY)

9.1   Reaffirmation Agreement

A REAFFIRMATION is an agreement between the debtor and a creditor that a particular debt will not be discharged in the bankruptcy case. This is most typically done with secured debts covering *personal property* such as motor vehicle loans. This is also done frequently with vehicle leases (called *executory agreements*). But in the case of a vehicle lease, the new contract or agreement will most likely be called an *assumption agreement*.

9.2   Statement of Intentions

It is the duty of each individual debtor that has secured debts to file a written statement of intentions with the court within 30 days of the bankruptcy filing. This statement sets out the debtor's intentions with respect to each secured debt and the property that secures the debt. Guess what? This document is called a *Statement of Intentions*.

The bankruptcy law says in effect that for each secured debt, the debtor must state that the debtor will:

- Surrender possession of the collateral to the creditor; or
- Reaffirm the debt and/or redeem the collateral.

Then, within 30 days after the first date set for the meeting of creditors, the debtor must actually **perform his or her intention.** (A conflicting provision of the law says that the debtor must surrender the collateral securing a debt with 45 days after the first meeting of creditors unless the debtor enters into a reaffirmation agreement or redeems the collateral. So the geniuses that so accurately named the Statement of Intentions missed the boat on explaining how it works. You'll have to discuss this with your lawyer.)

9.3   Performance of the Statement of Intentions

If the debtor fails to perform the required *"intention"* within 45 days after the first meeting of creditors, the automatic stay is terminated (goes away) with respect to any *personal property* securing the debt. Also, the Code says, "the creditor may take whatever action as to such property as is permitted under applicable nonbankruptcy law, unless the trustee timely seeks and obtains an order from the court requiring the debtor to surrender the property to the trustee."

What does this mean to a human? If you don't voluntarily give back the collateral (property) as you are supposed to do, or if you don't give the collateral to the trustee if he or she asks for it, then the creditor can come get it--provided they comply with state law. Now here's some particular technical information that you should also know about the repossession of such collateral.

Creditor's right to a nonbankruptcy law repossession. A creditor secured by personal property (not real estate) is free to repossess (take back) the collateral. This could be true even if the payments are current. How so? Well, what if you didn't maintain insurance on your vehicle? Stay with me here and read on.

Even when you are current on your payment to this creditor, you could lose the property if a situation exists that would have given the creditor the right to repossess in a case where a bankruptcy had never been filed. So you can see from the example above, since most motor vehicle financing agreements require the borrower to keep the vehicle insured, and to name the creditor on the insurance policy as a *loss payee,* you still have to comply with these contract terms or risk losing the car. Failure to carry the required insurance would be a material breach of that contract, allowing the creditor to repossess even though the monthly loan payments are current.

Likewise, most financing agreements state that the

insolvency of the borrower or a declaration of bankruptcy by the borrower is a material breach of the agreement. Most financing agreements provide that any material breach of the agreement allows the creditor to repossess. But if the debtor REAFFIRMS the agreement, then presumably the nonmonetary technical default triggered by the act of filing bankruptcy has been cured. But REAFFIRMATION requires an agreement of both the creditor and the debtor and it must be approved by the court (see below).

Nonmonetary breach and a creditor's right to repossession. Where the only breach of the agreement has been the technicality of the debtor filing Chapter 7, may the creditor repossess anyway? In other words, let's say that there is no failure to comply with any material contract provision except the clause that says you can't be insolvent or file bankruptcy. Will they still insist on repossessing the vehicle?

Most creditors (at least banks and other creditors in the motor vehicle financing business) have taken the position that *they will repossess* IF *the debtor fails to* REAFFIRM. They want the reaffirmation provisions of the new Bankruptcy Code to be strictly enforced.

This seems reasonable to them because in some cases they are rightly concerned that the debtor is going to abuse the vehicle then "walk" from the obligation as soon as it is convenient for the debtor to do so. Remember that your debt to that creditor gets DISCHARGED, so legally they can't sue you for the debt after bankruptcy even if you stayed current on your payments for a period of time after you file bankruptcy.

9.4   The Reaffirmation Process is Really a Big "Tug of War"

REAFFIRMATION creates a tension between the best interests of the debtor verses the best interests of the creditor. This makes sense if you just think about it a little bit.

It is usually serves the best interests of the creditor to keep the debtor *personally liable* for the obligation. So the creditor wants you to REAFFIRM the debt. But it is usually in best interests of the debtor to keep possession of personal property security (such as a motor vehicle) if it can be done without the personal liability that comes from a formal REAFFIRMATION agreement.

When the debtor keeps the collateral without making a REAFFIRMATION agreement, we call that a "ride thru" (because the debtor's continued possession of the collateral "rides thru" the bankruptcy and emerges intact at the end of the process minus any direct personal liability of the debtor). Pretty cool, huh?

9.5   Debtor's Advantages of a "Ride Through"

This is where the debtor keeps and enjoys the collateral (so long as the debtor keeps paying on time, and in the case of a motor vehicle, keeps it properly insured) but does not enter into a REAFFIRMATION agreement.

Essentially, a ride thru relieves the debtor from what used to be the ultimate detriment of every contract, namely, the personal liability for a *deficiency balance*. This is because the debtor's personal liability can be *discharged* in the bankruptcy, even though the creditor's lien stayed in place against the collateral.

In a ride thru situation, if the debtor fails to make payments in the future, then the debtor is protected from facing a lawsuit for any remaining contractual deficiency. For example, after repossession, a creditor is normally allowed to sell the collateral and then sue the borrower for any remaining loan balance after applying the proceeds received from the sale of the collateral. But not in the case of a ride thru since the debtor "discharged" that liability in the bankruptcy.

If the debtor finishes paying for the obligation, the lender must transfer title to the debtor.

The debtor is left free to walk away from the obligation at any time. This is an enormous advantage, because in effect it creates an escape clause that lets the debtor turn back the vehicle (or other collateral) any time that the debtor decides that it is no longer convenient to keep paying for it.

A subsequent default will still allow the creditor to repossess the collateral, but without a valid REAFFIRMATION agreement the creditor cannot also sue for a *deficiency balance*.

9.6 Can the Debtor Safely Ignore the Rule That Collateral Must Be Reaffirmed or Surrendered?

Prior to enactment the new bankruptcy law of 2005, case law concerning REAFFIRMATION agreements held that the collateral could not be repossessed so long as the debtor stayed current on the payments. So courts ignored or refused to enforce the nonmonetary default provisions in most contracts that are automatically triggered by filing bankruptcy. In effect, this allowed debtors to enjoy the "ride thru" without the detriment of continuing personal liability.

However, the provisions of the new bankruptcy law say that if the debtor fails to perform the required *"intention"* within 45 days after the first meeting of creditors, the automatic stay is terminated with respect to any *personal property* securing the obligation. And the Bankruptcy Code says, "the creditor may take whatever action as to such property as is permitted under applicable nonbankruptcy law," unless the trustee timely seeks and obtains an order from the court requiring the debtor to surrender the property to the trustee.

 *HUMAN TIP: Debtors take a big risk when they retain collateral without reaffirming the secured debt.* Until these issues are settled in the appellate courts, debtors are taking a big risk if they attempt to retain possession of collateral, especially vehicles, without reaffirming the debt.

9.7   Redemption

Redemption is a procedure in which the debtor seeks an order from the court allowing the debtor to buy the collateral by paying the collateral's value to the secured creditor. This can be very advantageous to the debtor, because the collateral is often worth a lot less than the amount of the loan.

For example, a car loan might have a $10,000 balance, but the car may actually be worth only $5000. Redemption allows the debtor to buy that car for what it is currently worth. The "catch" is that the debtor cannot force the creditor to accept installment payments of the redemption price. In other words, the redemption value must be paid in full at the time of redemption. And if the creditor and the debtor can't agree on the value of the collateral, then the debtor has to seek a court determination. This kind of court proceeding may require the assistance of an attorney and can be expensive.

HUMAN TIP: You may be able to negotiate with some creditors for better terms. Sometimes the debtor can negotiate with the creditor for better terms, such as a reduced interest rate and a significant reduction on the balance owed. This is common when the collateral consists of appliances, furniture and jewelry. But when the collateral is a motor vehicle, creditors generally require a REAFFIRMATION for the full balance unless the debtor is going to tender the cash redemption price in full.

9.8 Reaffirmations are Disfavored by Most Courts

The debtor's attorney and frequently the court itself will not want a debtor to be burdened with a REAFFIRMATION following the discharge of debts under Chapter 7. This is because it impedes the debtor's "*fresh start.*" For this reason the REAFFIRMATION of an unsecured debt such as a credit card balance or a medical debt is extremely rare.

9.9   Contents of Reaffirmation Form

If the debtor does not have an attorney—or if the debtor's lawyer will not be involved with the REAFFIRMATION agreement—then *the proposed form of agreement must be presented to the court for approval.* Most judges are very reluctant to approve such agreements and will search for a reason to deny them.

The REAFFIRMATION agreement form requires a disclosure of the current income and expenses of the debtor in order to show whether the debtor can actually afford the required payment. This form also contains mandatory language warning the debtor of the consequences of making the agreement. The agreement is required to disclose certain information, such as the amount of the debt that is being reaffirmed, the payment terms, interest rate, and the consequences of a default.

9.10   Lawyers Representing Debtors are Reluctant to Sign

One of the reasons for the reluctance of lawyers to participate in a REAFFIRMATION is simple. They generally believe that it's bad for their clients to do these agreements. Plus, they don't want to sign a declaration that the law requires if they participate.

The lawyer that assists the debtor with a REAFFIRMATION must sign a declaration under penalty of perjury stating that the REAFFIRMATION would not produce an undue hardship upon the debtor. Most attorneys take their responsibilities very seriously and they are reluctant to sign such a declaration and saddle their client with such obligations.

The reaffirmation becomes effective if signed by all of the parties and the debtor's attorney, and if it is filed with the court prior to discharge, unless it is *presumed to be an undue hardship*.

HUMAN TIP: Maybe you shouldn't be signing something that your own lawyer won't sign. Doesn't it tell you something important when your own lawyer refuses to sign the documents for a REAFFIRMATION? Many people in financially stressful situations are simply trying to "get by" or "hang on" to things that seem important. But when these same people have the perspective of time passing by, they begin to understand what was so obvious—that freedom from old debts and a truly "fresh start" is more important.

9.11 Reaffirmation and the Presumption of Undue Hardship

The REAFFIRMATION is *presumed to be an undue hardship* if the debtor's monthly expenses exceed the debtor's monthly income. In that event, the court must examine the agreement and *may* disapprove the agreement. The presumption may be rebutted by written evidence identifying additional sources of income that will allow the debtor to make the payments called for in the agreement. Interestingly, the *presumption* of *undue hardship* does not apply where the creditor is a *credit union.*

9.12 Reaffirmation Hearing

The Bankruptcy Code says there must be a court hearing to approve a REAFFIRMATION in a case where the debtor is not represented by an attorney. (*Bankruptcy Code Section 524.*) At this hearing, the court must inquire as to the circumstances surrounding the obligation and must determine whether or not the REAFFIRMATION would be an undue hardship upon the debtor or any dependent of the debtor.

The court will look at the current income and expenses of the debtor to see if the debtor can actually afford the required payment. The Bankruptcy Code states that the court must approve a reaffirmation as consistent with the debtor's best interests. For this reason, it appears that the court still holds the discretion to deny a REAFFIRMATION even if the debtor believes it is in his or her best interest to reaffirm.

Court approval of a REAFFIRMATION at a hearing is not required if the agreement is a reaffirmation of a mortgage securing real estate.

HUMAN TIP: Reaffirmation is a potential pitfall to avoid whenever possible. Reaffirmation of a debt is often a dangerous pitfall for the debtor, because some creditors will use subtle forms of coercion and intimidation to squeeze an unnecessary REAFFIRMATION out of the debtor. Reaffirmation leaves the debtor "on the hook" to pay a debt which would have been discharged. Particularly dangerous is any proposed reaffirmation of a mortgage.

9.13 Rescission of Reaffirmation

The debtor is entitled to *rescind* (erase) a REAFFIRMATION agreement during the following time period: (a) at any time prior to discharge; or (b) within sixty days after making the agreement, *whichever time period is longer.*

9.14 The Reaffirmation Process Creates Conflicts Between the Lawyer and Client

We'd like to walk you through a fairly common REAFFIRMATION scenario to show you how conflicts between the lawyer and client come about. We hope this will give potential debtors some perspective about the process.

Imagine that the client is demanding that his or her lawyer sign the client's proposed motor vehicle REAFFIRMATION agreement, and the lawyer does not want to do so. What are the lawyer and client thinking and why?

Reaffirmation from the lawyer's perspective:
The lawyer may know that the client has previously had

difficulty staying current on payments for the vehicle. The lawyer may also know from reviewing financial records that the client is prone to recurring financial hardships and irregular income.

The lawyer may be convinced that the client is going to default at some future date, losing the vehicle anyway. If the vehicle is repossessed, the client will also suffer a significant deficiency liability that could have been discharged in the bankruptcy.

The lawyer does not want to take any professional risk for letting the client sign a reaffirmation that may be prone to failure. The reaffirmation agreement requires the lawyer to sign a declaration under penalty of perjury that the agreement will not create an undue hardship. How can the lawyer really say that under oath?

The car is worth a lot less money than the amount of the debt and is really a bad deal all things considered.

The reaffirmation requirements impose duties on the lawyer that go far beyond what most lawyers feel is the appropriate role for an advocate. Most lawyers will resist this different role. They feel that the requirements force them to become what in effect is a character witness for their client because they must declare that the deal creates "no undue hardship" on their client!

Reaffirmation from the client's perspective.

The client is worried sick over the thought of losing his or her car and doesn't think there are any viable alternatives.

The client becomes frustrated by the lawyer's reluctance or actual refusal to sign the proposed agreement. If the lawyer does not sign the REAFFIRMATION agreement, it won't be effective unless the court holds a hearing and approves it.

A court reaffirmation hearing means the client may have to take a day off from work, face the anxiety of having to go to court, pay for parking at court, possibly pay their lawyer to go with them and advocate for an agreement that the lawyer actually disfavors, and still possibly face denial of the agreement by a judge who will be looking for an excuse to withhold approval.

All of this unpleasantness would be avoided if the lawyer would just sign the agreement.

The client feels that there is no risk that he or she would ever default (again).

The client believes that he or she has no choice and must reaffirm because he or she won't be able to get another car if this one is lost.

9.15 Alternatives for Avoiding a Bad Reaffirmation Agreement

Assume the debtor is faced with having to reaffirm a $10,000 loan balance for a vehicle worth only $5000, or else give up the wheels. In some cases there may be ways you can get around the Debtor's perceived need to accept a bad bargain that clearly is not in the debtor's best interests.

First ask, "Would you really like to buy this exact same vehicle all over again, in the present condition 'as is' for the same amount of money that you will already owe under this agreement? (Under this perspective, most clients will say "No way" and at least open their minds up to the possibility of other alternatives).

Here are some strategies that you might consider. We are

not judging the morality of these tactics. These are offered simply as emergency stop gaps to solve a temporary transportation issue so that the debtor does not get trapped in a bad reaffirmation.

IDEA 1: Stop making car payments and buy something cheap for cash.

As soon as the case is filed, the debtor ordinarily has a "free ride" under the automatic stay. This will ordinarily protect the vehicle from repossession for about two and one-half months (that is, until 45 days after the *first meeting of creditors*).

The debtor should use that time to save up money towards buying a cheap "transportation car" until the debtor is able to get into something else (see below). Very cheap cars really are available. With careful shopping, they can be had from private parties and from organizations. For example, both the Salvation Army and Goodwill sell cheap running cars that have been donated. They have several locations. (Note: A debtor that can't save enough money to buy themselves a "runner" vehicle will likely never have been able to make the payments on a reaffirmation.)

IDEA 2: Buy a car with financing after bankruptcy.

Upon discharge, most debtors are aggressively solicited by new car dealers, offering "easy terms" to finance or lease a new car. They specifically target people emerging from bankruptcy as sales leads. The debtor can usually get into a new car, even with bad credit, provided they have a sufficient and steady income. This may be a far better alternative than making a bad reaffirmation.

The new car loan won't start out with more money owing than the vehicle is worth, it likely will represent a better investment than keeping the debtor's old car with upside down financing on it. It's also likely that the new car will probably be more reliable transportation with a new car warranty.

Of course, the catch is that the debtor needs to play for time to get their discharge. Here is how to do that: Reaffirm if necessary to keep temporary possession of the vehicle until the debtor receives a discharge, but rescind the reaffirmation within 60 days after discharge (or within the applicable time limit—see above). Use that time to get into another vehicle, and be sure to rescind the reaffirmation before it becomes binding.

IDEA 3: Get help from a friend.

Maybe a friend, lover or family member will buy or lease something for the debtor to drive? The debtor can be insured and registered as a driver of the vehicle, and the debtor can be the one who makes the payments.

IDEA 4: Rent or borrow while waiting for your discharge.

There are companies that will rent used cars on a monthly

basis. The payment for these monthly rentals is usually much less than the payments on the debtor's car loan. After the debtor receives a discharge the debtor can probably purchase and finance a new car.

IDEA 5: Use public transportation while waiting for your discharge.

Maybe there is public transportation that the debtor can use on a temporary basis, until discharge, and then buy a new car?

10

DEBTS NOT AFFECTED BY DISCHARGE

10.1 Nondischargeable Debts

Chapter 7 bankruptcy does not discharge every kind of debt. The Bankruptcy Code (in Section 523) sets out a laundry list of different types of obligations that are not dischargeable. The best way to understand the likely difference between the dischargeable debts (the ones you are "released from") and the nondischargeable debts (the ones the you are stuck with) is to think of acts committed by the debtor which amount to intentional wrongs (intentional torts). Generally, intentional acts of wrongdoing, such as *fraud*, are not dischargeable.

10.2 Public Policy

Other types of debts which are not going to be dischargeable are debts that have a very important social aspect to them, separate and apart from the monetary amount which the obligation represents. These include debts such as *taxes, student loans, alimony, spouse support and child support.*

You can attach a dollar amount to these debts, but they also have a social element that is extremely important to society at large. The public policy of every state is that persons must support their children. They must support the spouses when ordered to do so. They must pay their taxes and they must pay back their student loans. So the Bankruptcy Code very clearly provides that most of those kinds of societal obligations are not going to be discharged. In addition, Chapter 7 does not discharge debts arising from a divorce or marital separation agreement (for example a property division or equalization judgment).

10.3 An Exception for Discharging Some Income Taxes

Taxes owed to the United States or any state, county, or other governmental entities are normally nondischargeable. However, *income taxes* will discharge if all of the following criteria are met:

- The taxes are more than three years old at the time the Bankruptcy was filed. (The three-year period begins to run from the time the returns were due, plus any periods of extension);

- If the return was not filed on time, more than two years has expired since the return was filed;
- If there was an assessment, more than 240 days have expired from the date of the assessment before the bankruptcy is filed;
- There has been no fraud.

HUMAN TIP: Get accurate information about your tax debts and important dates.
If you intend to discharge taxes with your bankruptcy filing, we recommend that you obtain a complete history of your tax obligations for each specific year in question from the IRS and consult a tax professional before filing the bankruptcy. To get your Federal IRS tax history, call the IRS at 800-829-1040 and ask them for a report called MFTRA-X. Tell them you want the MFTRA-X for each year for which you owe taxes. They will mail you the reports; and they might even fax them if you ask them nicely. Also note that a bankruptcy discharge does not automatically remove any filed or recorded tax lien on any property which you own.

10.4 Discharging Student Loans

Student loans are generally not dischargeable if they are guaranteed by or partly funded by a government entity or a nonprofit institution. This includes any student loan that carries payments which are qualified under the IRS Code for income tax deductibility.

However, under some circumstances these loans may be

discharged on a showing that they would impose an undue hardship on the debtor and dependents of the debtor. Unfortunately, to make this showing of undue hardship, there is a process that is extremely difficult for most debtors. The process involves filing a lawsuit against the creditor and in this lawsuit the debtor has the burden of proof. Such suits are very complicated and time consuming to pursue. They require the assistance of legal counsel which can be very expensive.

10.4 Undue Hardship Student Loan Discharge

Court decisions that find undue hardship for the debtor have been extremely rare in the reported case decisions. The reported cases that grant such a hardship typically do so for individuals that suffer from some type of very severe permanent and total disability or some sort of permanent disability that drastically restricts the ability of the debtor to earn more than a subsistence level of income. The courts require a finding that the debtor has proven each of the following three elements of undue hardship:

1. That the debtor cannot maintain, based upon current income and expenses, a "minimal" standard of living for himself and his dependents if compelled to repay the student loans; **and**
2. That additional circumstances exist indicating that this state of affairs is likely to persist for a significant portion of the repayment period of

the student loans; **and**

3. That the debtor has made good faith efforts to repay the student loans.

PART III:
HOW CHAPTER 13 WORKS

11

WHY CHOOSE A CHAPTER 13

11.1 Drawbacks of Chapter 7

Chapter 7 provides a fairly wide range of debt relief for a prospective debtor but it does not do all things for all people. There are some debt problems that Chapter 7 just does not help. These are typically situations where the debtor's assets (a house or a car, for example) have loans against them that are behind in payments.

A Chapter 7 case will temporarily stop a foreclosure on your home, but the filing of the case and the imposition of the automatic stay does not allow the debtor to force a creditor into accepting a payment schedule for the cure of the defaulted payment amounts.

When the Chapter 7 is discharged the automatic stay normally ends. It could end sooner where the creditor files a motion to lift the stay. This frees a secured creditor to proceed with lien enforcement and lets them pick up where they left off when the bankruptcy was filed. In other words, they are free to finish the foreclosure. Also, in some California foreclosure cases, the automatic stay will not stop the running of the statutory time that the borrower has under state law to cure a default.

In the case of an automobile loan that is delinquent, the vehicle will eventually be repossessed. Thus, Chapter 7 is an imperfect remedy for individuals who have defaulted on secured obligations and who want to keep the collateral (the asset affected by the lien).

11.2   Typical Chapter 13 Cases

Historically, the typical Chapter 13 case is filed by someone trying to stop the foreclosure sale of their home. The balance of Chapter 13 cases are probably filed by individuals who are trying to reorganize tax debts, deal with a default situation on motor vehicles, or retain nonexempt assets that would be liquidated if the case was administered under Chapter 7. Of course, now that the new bankruptcy law applies, there are some Chapter 13 filings by individuals who have been excluded from a Chapter 7 because of the Means Test.

12

CHAPTER 13 CAN CURE A DEFAULT

12.1 Stop a Foreclosure

In the case of a real estate foreclosure, the debtor files the Chapter 13 case which imposes an immediate automatic stay and stops the foreclosure. This must be done *before the foreclosure auction* takes place and notice of the automatic stay needs to be given to the necessary parties.

12.2 Plan to Cure the Default

Once the Chapter 13 case is filed, the debtor must do something to "cure" the default on the loan. The "cure" comes through a Plan. The Plan takes a little time to propose and to get confirmed by the court, so what happens in the meantime?

Well, the court is not going to simply let the debtor sit there and enjoy the benefits of property ownership without the burden of making payments. So what actually happens under the Chapter 13 law and the local rules of the bankruptcy court is that the debtor must immediately begin making regular monthly payments again on the mortgage.

Payments must commence with the next payment that comes due following the filing of the bankruptcy case. Then it is up to the debtor's Plan to demonstrate how the defaulted amounts will be "caught up" or paid.

12.3 Gradual Cure of Default

The best way to understand the process is to think of it as if the debtor is drawing a line in the sand. The debtor says, "I am buried up to my neck in debt and delinquent payments; I am not going to go any deeper in the hole; I am going to start making regular monthly payments and in addition to that I will pay some extra money to gradually catch myself up."

It is the payment of those extra monies that will allow the debtor to cure the default on his or her property over a reasonable period of time. The concept is really fairly simple although in practice it can become quite complicated.

13

CHAPTER 13 CAN "CRAM DOWN" A CREDITOR

13.1 Cram Down

A Plan in Chapter 13 may be used to force a secured creditor to accept an "adjusted" debt amount and take lower payments over time. This is most often used to adjust debts on motor vehicles and other personal property collateral such as furniture and appliances. Let's see how this works using a motor vehicle loan as an example.

13.2 Example -- Motor Vehicles

Suppose the debtor possesses a car worth $5,000.00 but there is $10,000.00 owed against it. Let's also suppose the debtor is running two, three, four months behind on their automobile payments and the car is about to get repossessed. Again the filing of the Chapter 13 case will immediately protect the debtor's possession of the collateral and stop the repossession. And in the Plan, the debtor may propose payments to the creditor for the current market value of that automobile without regard to the actual contractual balance.

In this example, the debtor may propose a plan to pay the creditor the $5,000.00 (the current market value of the vehicle) and to pay that to the creditor in installments over a period that usually is going to be 36 months. This is the *secured value* of the lien.

We call this process a *"cram down"* because the secured claim has been forcibly "adjusted" down (or "crammed down") to the current value of the collateral. The law does require that the debtor must pay some interest to the creditor. Interest will be paid on the secured claim ($5,000) to compensate the creditor for the value of the delay in collecting the current market value of the automobile. However, the interest rate is often reduced below what the contract rate was originally.

 *HUMAN TIP.* There is an exception to cram down on motor vehicles.

An important exception to the "cram down" rules was included with the new bankruptcy law (2005). Under the new law, the debtor may not force a "cram down" on a secured purchase money motor vehicle obligation that was incurred within 910 days prior to the bankruptcy filing. However, the cram down should still be effective on any non-motor vehicle obligations, such as appliances and furniture.

14

THE CHAPTER 13 PLAN

The Plan is really the fine work of the Chapter 13 case. It is the road map that tells the court and the creditors where the case is going, at least as proposed by the debtor. The bankruptcy code requires that every debtor file a plan within 15 days after commencement of the case.

The plan must describe in some detail the method by which the debtor proposes to handle all of the debts. The law separates debts into "classes" that are recognized and required by law. The Plan sets out these classes or groupings so creditors understand how the plan affects them. It identifies funding sources (typically income of the debtor) and the duration or time over which payments will be made. And it establishes which debts will be discharged and how that will occur. After the plan is proposed by the Debtor, it must go through a "Confirmation Process" where it must be approved by the bankruptcy court. So let's take a look at these parts of the Plan and the process.

14.1 Classification of Debts

Priority claims.

The typical plan should divide the debts into logical categories, including the categories or "classes" required by law. For example, certain debts are required under the Bankruptcy Code to be paid or satisfied in full (such as non-dischargeable tax obligations) and these are typically going to be put under a priority classification along with family support obligations. This "priority" class of debts might also contain a provision for payment of the debtor's attorney fees.

Attorney's fees.

A large percentage of debtors will pay all or most of their attorney's fees for their legal representation as a component of the Chapter 13 plan. The plan also will divide debts into other logical categories such as a category for general unsecured claims without priority, a category for secured claims which are secured by the debtor's home (principal residence), perhaps a category for secured claims secured by collateral other than the debtor's principal residence, perhaps a category of claims for debts that are secured by personal property such as motor vehicles, big screen TV's and other appliances.

Secured claims.

A general requirement for Plans is that the debtor must

pay interest to the creditor on the value of the secured portion of such claims. The separation of classes makes it easier for the court and creditors to understand the different ways these "classes" of claims are "treated" under the Plan.

14.2 Duration of the Plan

No plan is allowed to extend beyond the duration of 60 months. If the debtor enjoys an *above-median income* level, the plan duration, called a *"commitment period"* is required by law to be 60 months (less only if the plan pays all claims in full) so as to maximize any possible repayment to unsecured creditors.

Otherwise, the commitment period is 36 months for those with *below-median income*, unless there is *"cause"* to extend the duration for up to 60 months total duration. *"Cause"* to extend beyond 36 months has been found where the debtor voluntarily desires to pay more to creditors or where the debtor can't afford to complete the required payments (such as payments to secured claims and priority claims) within 36 months.

15

CHAPTER 13 PLAN -- THE CONFIRMATION PROCESS

15.1 The Debtor Must Prove Feasibility and Good Faith

A debtor must establish at least two important things to have a Plan confirmed by the Court. The debtor must provide the court some convincing evidence or proof that the plan is "feasible" and that the plan is proposed in "good faith."

Feasibility and good faith are extremely important components of the confirmation (adjudication) of a Chapter 13 plan. For example: if the debtor does not have sufficient regular income in order to meet his or her own regular ordinary living expenses and to make the payments that are called for under the plan, there is a serious problem; that plan is not feasible unless it is to be funded from the sale of certain property in a reasonable way.

15.2 Evidence of Regular Income

There is no reason why the court should delay the creditors any longer from taking possession of collateral when the debtor has no ability to fund the plan that is being proposed. The debtor is required to present the court with copies of pay stubs and other documents to establish current regular income for the 60 day period prior to the bankruptcy filing, along with copies of tax returns for the past 4 years. This is to prove that the debtor has *regular income*.

15.3 Other Funding Sources

Sometimes a debtor will propose funding the plan with sources of income that come from third parties, for example the income of roommates, domestic life partners, other individuals or family members who perhaps live with the debtor and contribute to the expenses of the common household.

In these situations the court will usually require that the debtor present some sort of evidence, usually in the form of a declaration signed by the third party. This declaration must attest to the fact that the third party does intend to make the financial contributions that are called for in the plan and also that they have the ability to do so. To prove their ability to contribute, the third party will typically be required to present some evidence of current regular income so that the court will be certain that there is every reasonable prospect that the Plan payments being proposed are actually going to be paid by the debtor.

15.4 Eligibility

Another key requirement of every Chapter 13 plan is that the debtor is eligible for the relief available under Chapter 13. Section 109(e) of the Bankruptcy Code establishes the criteria for debtor eligibility. Debtor eligibility under Chapter 13 is limited to individuals with regular income who have non contingent liquidated unsecured debts which total less than $383,175, and non-contingent liquidated secured debt not exceeding $1,149,525. These dollar limits are those in effect on April 1, 2013 and are adjusted periodically to reflect changes in the Consumer Price Index.

16

CHAPTER 13 -- THE DISCHARGE OF DEBT

16.1 Basic Discharge

When the debtor completes a Chapter 13 case, the discharge eliminates all of the remaining balances owed on all general unsecured debts (those debts without priority) that were provided for in the Plan.

Those unsecured debts will by then already have received payment based on what the debtor could reasonably afford. One limitation that affects a Chapter 13 Plan is that it must pay those unsecured debts at least as much as the creditors would have received if the debtors nonexempt assets had instead been liquidated under chapter 7. Sometimes this will be payment in full; sometimes it will be a percentage of the claims; sometimes it may even be nothing (under the right circumstances).

16.2 Distinctions in Discharge Between Chapter 7 and Chapter 13

The new bankruptcy law in 2005 brought changes to the area of a Chapter 13 discharge. Previously, the Chapter 13 discharge was much broader than the Chapter 7 discharge. The discharge of debts provided for under Chapter 13 is still broader than the discharge under chapter 7, but the new bankruptcy law (2005) has narrowed the differences considerably.

With minor exceptions, debts that are nondischargeable under Chapter 7 have now been made nondischargeable under Chapter 13. The main exceptions to this are that Chapter 13 will discharge debts (other than debts in the nature of *support*) that arise from a divorce or separation agreement. It will also discharge debts that arise from a *willful or malicious injury* caused by the debtor (unless there has already been *restitution* or *damages awarded* in a *civil action* against the debtor).

16.3 The Hardship Discharge -- When Bad Things Happen That Interrupt Your Plan

After confirmation of a plan, circumstances may arise that prevent the debtor from completing the plan. In such situations, the debtor may ask the court to grant a **hardship discharge**. 11 U.S.C. § 1328(b).

Generally, a hardship discharge is available only if:

- the debtor's failure to complete plan payments is due to circumstances beyond the debtor's control and through no fault of the debtor; and
- creditors have received at least as much as they would have received in a chapter 7 liquidation case; and
- modification of the plan is not possible.

Injury or illness that prevents employment sufficient to fund even a modified plan may serve as the basis for a hardship discharge. The hardship discharge is more limited than the discharge described above and does not apply to any debts that are nondischargeable in a chapter 7 case. 11 U.S.C. § 523.

EXTRA
FEATURES

EXTRA FEATURES

GLOSSARY OF KEY TERMS

AUTOMATIC STAY

A restraining order against your creditors which takes effect immediately and automatically when you file a petition under the bankruptcy laws. In most cases this stops bill collectors from bothering  you. It also stops lawsuits, foreclosures, even the IRS; and it creates a cooling off period while the court system sorts things out. It is not permanent and in some cases creditors may be given relief from the automatic stay to seize collateral that you will not keep or cannot afford after bankruptcy.

BANKRUPTCY SCHEDULES

Detailed lists filed by the debtor along with (or shortly after filing) the petition showing the debtor's assets, debts, and other financial information. There are official forms for these Schedules that debtors must use.

BAPCPA

This stands for the Bankruptcy Abuse Prevention and Consumer Protection Act of 2005. Commonly referred to as the "New Bankruptcy Law", BAPCPA attempts to, among other things, make it more difficult for some consumers to file bankruptcy under Chapter 7, but some of these consumers may instead utilize Chapter 13.

CERTIFIED BANKRUPTCY SPECIALIST

California has a legal certification program for Bankruptcy Specialists (as well as 10 other areas of law) that is designed to protect the public. This program requires attorneys to demonstrate high competence and experience through testing and evaluations in bankruptcy by an objective certification panel. More information is available to consumers at the California State Bar website: http://ls.calbar.ca.gov/.

CHAPTER 7

The Chapter of the Bankruptcy Code that provides a procedure for debtors to receive a discharge from their debts and get a "fresh start." As part of this procedure, the debtor gets to keep exempt (protected) property but must give up non-exempt (unprotected) property. The unprotected property is sold (liquidated) by the trustee and this is why this Chapter is often referred to as a "liquidation."

CHAPTER 13

The chapter of the Bankruptcy Code provides a system and rules for the adjustment of debts of individuals with regular income. Chapter 13 allows a debtor to keep property and pay debts over time, usually three to five years.

CONSUMER DEBTS

Debts incurred for personal, family or household needs as opposed to business needs.

CURRENT MONTHLY INCOME ("CMI")

The average monthly income of the debtor over the six calendar months before the filing of the bankruptcy case. This includes regular contributions to household expenses from nondebtors and income from the debtor's spouse if the petition is a joint petition. But it does not include social security income and certain other payments made because the debtor is the victim of certain crimes.

DEBTOR

In consumer cases, this is the individual (or "human") that files bankruptcy. A husband and wife may file a single petition as "joint debtors."

DENIAL OF DISCHARGE

An order from the bankruptcy court that denies the relief from debts normally given in a discharge.

DISCHARGE

A permanent order from the bankruptcy court enjoining creditors from trying ever again to collect on a debt that has been properly disclosed and is subject to discharge in your bankruptcy case. This order acts as a "release" from personal liability from these debts. Most debts are "dischargeable" in your case and will be subject to the DISCHARGE order, but there are some exceptions. In cases of abuse, it is possible for the bankruptcy court to bar or deny your DISCHARGE, so complying with the law and avoiding pre-bankruptcy or post-bankruptcy abuse of the laws is crucial.

DISMISSAL

An order from the bankruptcy court that dismisses your bankruptcy case. If your case is dismissed, there may be negative consequences in your later bankruptcy case if you choose to re-file a petition.

EXEMPTIONS

Bankruptcy exemptions determine what property you get to keep in a Chapter 7 case, whether it is your home, car, pension, personal belongings, or other property. If property is "exempt," you may keep it during and after bankruptcy. If property is non-exempt, the trustee is entitled to sell it to pay your unsecured creditors. In Chapter 13, exemptions help determine how much you will have to pay to unsecured creditors through your Chapter 13 plan.

Figuring out which bankruptcy exemptions to use and

how to use them is one of the most challenging parts of filing for bankruptcy because bankruptcy law is a confusing mixture of federal and state law. Each state has a set of exemptions that apply in bankruptcy. Most states require you to use those state exemptions. However, seventeen states allow debtors to choose between the state exemption system and another set of exemptions created by Congress, called the federal bankruptcy exemptions. California is unique in that it has two sets of state exemptions that debtors may choose from. If you have a choice of exemption systems, you must choose one system or the other. You cannot mix and match.

FRAUDULENT TRANSFERS

Title or ownership transfers or gifts of assets made be debtors before bankruptcy that are deemed unfair or that were made in an attempt to hide assets or remove assets from the reach of your creditors. The trustee in your bankruptcy case has the power to sue you and the people that received these transfers (using bankruptcy law and state laws). The trustee is allowed to get the assets back or get a money judgment for the value of the assets you attempted to remove from your creditors grasp. And if this occurs, you will also lose the right to claim any exemptions to protect value in these assets if those exemptions were available to you.

HYPOTHETICAL LIVING EXPENSES

A combination of national and local expense standards updated annually from statistics and calculations published by the IRS. These hypothetical expenses are complicated and they are part of the calculations your bankruptcy attorney (or the court) must use in applying the Means Test to your circumstances to determine how much leftover or net income you have. But note that these expenses are "hypothetical" so they could be accurate to your circumstances or above or below your actual expenses by category. This is one of the reasons that practitioners consider the Means Test to be unfair and arbitrary. You can find the standards that will apply to you at the website maintained by the Department of Justice and the United States Trustee program. (See Other Bankruptcy Resources at the back of this book.)

MEANS TEST

A calculation required by the bankruptcy law that is meant to determine if a Chapter 7 filing is presumed to be an abuse of the law. If you can't pass the Means Test, your bankruptcy is dismissed or you have the option to continue in Chapter 13.

The Means Test calculation begins by combining a person's real living expenses with certain hypothetical living expenses established by the government. For example, the allowed expense for rent for a single person in Los Angeles County is $1,832 regardless of whether you pay more or less than this. The combined real and hypothetical expenses are then subtracted from a person's six months average gross income (not including the month of the bankruptcy filing) to see if there is any "projected disposable income" left over to pay creditors. If there would be any leftover income, the law says abuse is presumed if the "leftover" amount is enough to pay general creditors during a 60 month time period approximately $150 a month.

MEDIAN INCOME

A standard of income used in the Means Test that is determined on a regional basis from Federal Census data. The Median Income that applies to your case will depend on the circumstances of your case, such as the number of earners and size of household. The actual tables for the income levels may be found at the website maintained by the Department of Justice and the United States Trustee program. (See Other Bankruptcy Resources at the back of this book.)

NON-EXEMPT ASSETS

Assets that are not protected in bankruptcy. If these assets have value, they may be taken by the Trustee and sold in order to raise money to pay creditors. Value includes "net value" or "equity" over and above the liens on the asset.

PETITION

The initial court paper, combined with schedules and other documents, which is filed to begin a case under the bankruptcy laws. It is your official request to the court for help in resolving your debt problems.

PLAN

In Chapter 13, the plan is a debtor's detailed description of how the debtor proposes to pay creditors' claims over a fixed period of time, usually three to five years.

PRE-BANKRUPTCY PLANNING

The arrangement (or rearrangement) of a debtor's property to allow the debtor to take maximum advantage of exemptions. Prebankruptcy planning typically includes converting nonexempt assets into exempt assets when this is allowed by law. This planning should be done with a certified bankruptcy specialist.

PREFERENTIAL TRANSFERS

Certain payments or other transfers of property to creditors that occur prior to bankruptcy, but within the "preference periods" provided by law. The normal preference period is 90 days, but a one year preference period applies to relatives or "insiders" of the debtor. There is a complex set of rules that applies to preferences and not all transfers or payments within the time periods will result in a "preference."

PROJECTED DISPOSABLE INCOME

This is a calculation that is part of the Means Test to determine eligibility to file Chapter 7 and to avoid a determination of "abuse." It is the amount of money left over after subtracting a combination of real and hypothetical living expenses from the debtors Current Monthly Income (CMI).

REAFFIRMATION

An agreement between a Chapter 7 debtor to continue paying a dischargeable debt (such as an auto loan) after the bankruptcy, usually for the purpose of keeping collateral (i.e. the car) that would otherwise be subject to repossession. There are special rules that apply to how these agreements may be properly entered into and courts tend to disfavor them since they go against the basic bankruptcy premise of a "fresh start."

REORGANIZATION

In consumer cases, a Chapter 13 case that allows debtors with regular income to adjust debts, keep property and pay the adjusted debts over time, usually three to five years.

TRUSTEE

The representative of the bankruptcy estate who exercises legal powers, principally for the benefit of the unsecured creditors, under the general supervision of the court. The trustee is appointed and supervised by the U.S. trustee or bankruptcy administrator.

The trustee is a private individual appointed in all Chapter 7 and Chapter 13 cases. The trustee's responsibilities include reviewing the debtor's petition and schedules and bringing actions against creditors or the debtor to recover property of the bankruptcy estate. In Chapter 7, the trustee sells property of the estate and makes distributions to creditors. Trustees in Chapter 13 have similar duties to a Chapter 7 trustee and the additional responsibilities of overseeing the debtor's Reorganization plan, receiving payments from debtors, and disbursing plan payments to creditors.

OTHER BANKRUPTCY RESOURCES

 In addition to the many resources directly available in <u>A Human Guide to Bankruptcy</u> as well as our websites, blog and associated consumer books and materials, the links below may help consumers looking for specific information about the bankruptcy process. These resources are provided either for citation or reference only, and we do not promote, take responsibility for or control the completeness, accuracy or timeliness of the content on any such websites.

Median Income Tables - Census Bureau Median Family Income By Family Size
www.justice.gov/ust/eo/bapcpa/20110315/bci_data/median_income_table.htm

US Trustee Program
www.justice.gov/ust/index.htm

US Trustee Consumer Information
www.justice.gov/ust/eo/public_affairs/consumer_info/index.htm

US Trustee Program – Means Testing
www.justice.gov/ust/eo/bapcpa/20061001/meanstesting.htm

U.S. Justice Dept. national and local expense

standards based on IRS collection standards
www.justice.gov/ust/eo/bapcpa/meanstesting.htm

US Bankruptcy Court, Central District of California
www.cacb.uscourts.gov

United States Federal Courts – Bankruptcy Resources
www.uscourts.gov/FederalCourts/Bankruptcy.aspx

US Trustee Information for people with Limited English Proficiency
www.justice.gov/ust/eo/public_affairs/lep/index.htm

Spanish language information (from US Trustee) about bankruptcy
www.justice.gov/ust/eo/ust_org/bky-info/docs/bky-info_spanish.pdf

Consumer facts about Credit Counseling from the Federal Trade Commission
www.justice.gov/ust/eo/bapcpa/ccde/docs/FTC_Consu Con_AlertCC.pdf

California Exemptions that apply in Bankruptcy Cases
http://www.courts.ca.gov/documents/ej156.pdf

LOS ANGELES AREA BANKRUPTCY COURT LOCATIONS

COURT DIVISION - STREET ADDRESS	TELEPHONE
Los Angeles Division: U.S. Bankruptcy Court 255 E. Temple Street Los Angeles, CA 90012	(213) 894-3118
Riverside Division: U.S. Bankruptcy Court 3420 Twelfth Street Riverside, CA 92501	(951) 774-1000
Santa Ana Division: U.S. Bankruptcy Court 411 West Fourth Street Santa Ana, CA 92701	(714) 338-5300
Santa Barbara Division: U.S. Bankruptcy Court 1415 State Street Santa Barbara, CA 93101	(805) 884-4800
San Fernando Valley Division: U.S. Bankruptcy Court 21041 Burbank Boulevard Woodland Hills, CA 91367	(818) 587-2900

CURRENT DOLLAR AMOUNTS OF CALIFORNIA EXEMPTIONS

Code of Civil Procedure sections 703.140(b) and 704.010 et seq.

Back in Chapter 5 we told you about the way EXEMPTIONS work in bankruptcy cases. We also told you that without advice from an expert bankruptcy lawyer, these lists are not enough to plan your bankruptcy case. But we thought you'd like to see the lists anyway. So here they are (with one more caution)!

The following lists of exemptions are included as a matter of convenience--for illustration purposes only--and the amounts are subject to change, so always check with an expert before you proceed.

Be aware also that these exemptions apply in California and have application in bankruptcy where California exemptions may apply. But you will absolutely need advice (told you so) and help from a qualified lawyer that is a certified specialist in bankruptcy law in California in order to determine which exemptions are right for your situation, and also to determine how to claim these exemptions in a bankruptcy case.

Exemptions Under Section 703.140(b)

The following lists the current dollar amounts of

exemptions from enforcement of judgment under Code of Civil Procedure section 703.140(b). These amounts are effective April 1, 2013. Unless otherwise provided by statute after that date, they will be adjusted at each three-year interval, ending on March 31. The amount of the adjustment to the prior amounts is based on the change in the annual California Consumer Price Index for All Urban Consumers for the most recent three-year period ending on the preceding December 31, with each adjusted amount rounded to the nearest $25. (See Code Civ. Proc., § 703.150(d).)

CURRENT DOLLAR AMOUNTS OF CALIFORNIA EXEMPTIONS THAT APPLY IN BANKRPUTCY CASES IF PROPERLY CLAIMED
Code of Civil Proc. sections 703.140(b)

CCP §703.140(b)	Type of Property	Amount of Exemption
(1)	The debtor's aggregate interest in real property or personal property that the debtor or a dependent of the debtor uses as a residence, or in a cooperative that owns property that the debtor or a dependent of the debtor uses as a residence	$25,575
(2)	The debtor's interest in one or more motor vehicles	$5,100
(3)	The debtor's interest in household furnishings, household goods, wearing apparel, appliances, books, animals, crops, or musical	$650

**CURRENT DOLLAR AMOUNTS OF CALIFORNIA
EXEMPTIONS THAT APPLY IN BANKRPUTCY CASES IF
PROPERLY CLAIMED**
Code of Civil Proc. sections 703.140(b)

instruments, that are held primarily
for the personal, family, or
household use of the debtor or a
dependent of the debtor (value is of
any particular item)

(4)   The debtor's aggregate interest in $1,525
        jewelry held primarily for the
        personal, family, or household use
        of the debtor or a dependent of the
        debtor

(5)   The debtor's aggregate interest, plus $1,350
        any unused amount of the
        exemption provided under
        paragraph (1), in any property. (A
        total of $26,925 is available here if
        you add the full amount the
        "paragraph (1)" amount of $25,575.)

(6)   The debtor's aggregate interest in $7,625
        any implements, professional books,
        or tools of the trade of the debtor or
        the trade of a dependent of the
        debtor

(8)   The debtor's aggregate interest in $13,675
        any accrued dividend or interest
        under, or loan value of, any
        unmatured life insurance contract
        owned by the debtor under which
        the insured is the debtor or an

**CURRENT DOLLAR AMOUNTS OF CALIFORNIA
EXEMPTIONS THAT APPLY IN BANKRPUTCY CASES IF
PROPERLY CLAIMED**
Code of Civil Proc. sections 703.140(b)

individual of whom the debtor is a
dependent

(11)(D)	The debtor's right to receive, or property traceable to, a payment on account of personal bodily injury of the debtor or an individual of whom the debtor is a dependent	$25,575

Exemptions Under Section 704.010 et seq.

The following lists the current dollar amounts of exemptions from enforcement of judgment under title 9, division 2, chapter 4, article 3 (commencing with section 704.010) of the California Code of Civil Procedure (CCP).

These amounts are effective April 1, 2013. Unless otherwise provided by statute after that date, they will be adjusted at each three-year interval, ending on March 31. The amount of the adjustment to the prior amounts is based on the change in the annual California Consumer Price Index for All Urban Consumers for the most recent three-year period ending on the preceding December 31, with each adjusted amount rounded to the nearest $25. (See CCP § 703.150(d).)

CURRENT DOLLAR AMOUNTS OF CALIFORNIA EXEMPTIONS THAT APPLY IN BANKRUPTCY CASES IF PROPERLY CLAIMED
Code of Civil Proc. sections 704.010 et seq.

CCP §	Type of Property	Amount of Exemption
704.010	Motor vehicle (any combination of aggregate equity, proceeds of execution sale, and proceeds of insurance or other indemnification for loss, damage, or destruction)	$2,900
704.020	Household furnishings, appliances, provisions, wearing apparel and other personal effects which are ordinarily and reasonably necessary	No specific dollar limit
704.030	Material to be applied to repair or maintenance of residence	$3,050
704.040	Jewelry, heirlooms, art	$7,625
704.060	Personal property used in debtor's or debtor's spouse's trade, business, or profession (amount of exemption for commercial motor vehicle not to exceed $4,850)	$7,625
704.060	Personal property used in debtor's and spouse's common trade, business, or profession (amount of exemption for commercial motor vehicle not to exceed	$15,250

**CURRENT DOLLAR AMOUNTS OF CALIFORNIA
EXEMPTIONS THAT APPLY IN BANKRUPTCY CASES IF
PROPERLY CLAIMED**
Code of Civil Proc. sections 704.010 et seq.

$9,700)

704.080   Deposit account with direct
           payment of social security or
           public benefits (exemption
           without claim, section 704.080(b))
           [Note 1]

• Public benefits, one depositor is designated payee		$1,525
• Social security benefits, one depositor is designated payee		$3,050
• Public benefits, two or more depositors are designated payees [Note 2]		$2,275
• Social security benefits, two or more depositors are designated payees [Note 2]		$4,575

704.090   Inmate trust account $1,525

           Inmate trust account (restitution $300
           fine or order)   [See Note 3]

704.100   Aggregate loan value of $12,200
           unmatured life insurance policies

704.730(a)(1) Up to this amount of equity in the $75,0000
           home if debtor is single

           * *See the next section titled "The*

CURRENT DOLLAR AMOUNTS OF CALIFORNIA EXEMPTIONS THAT APPLY IN BANKRUPTCY CASES IF PROPERLY CLAIMED
Code of Civil Proc. sections 704.010 et seq.

California Homestead Exemption" for a human discussion of what this important exemption in California means and how it might apply to you.

704.730(a)(2)	Up to this amount of equity in the home if debtor is married or a qualified member of a family unit resides in the home	$100,000
704.730(a)(3)	Up to this amount of equity in the home for (A) person 65 years old or older; (B) person is physically or mentally disabled and can't engage in substantial gainful employment; or (C) person 55 years of age or older where annual income is $25,000 or less, or if married, joint income is $35,000 or less	$175,000

Note 1: The amount of a deposit account that exceeds exemption amounts is also exempt to the extent it consists of payments of public benefits or social security benefits. (Code Civ. Proc., § 704.080(c).)

Note 2: If only one joint payee is a beneficiary of the payment, the exemption is in the amount available to a single designated payee. (Code Civ. Proc., § 704.080(b)(3) and (4).)

Note 3: This amount is not subject to adjustments under Code Civ. Proc., § 703.150.

THE CALIFORNIA HOMESTEAD EXEMPTION

What is the California Homestead Exemption?

You've probably heard that there is "homestead" protection for your home. Well, let's see what that really means. California law protects a certain amount of "equity" or value in your home from attachment by creditors and this protection also applies in bankruptcy cases. This particular protection is found at Sec. Sec. 704.730 of the Calif. Code of Civil Procedure which is referenced in the Exemption tables in the back of this book.

However, this particular protection will only be available to debtors that choose all their exemptions from the California exemption list that begins at Sec. 704 of the Calif. Code of Civil Procedure. If it makes more sense for you to use the "other list" of exemptions (beginning at Code of Civil Procedure section 703.140(b)--see the earlier exemption tables), then there is a smaller exemption amount that is still available to protect some equity in real estate (up to $25,575).

But in many cases, debtors wish to protect significant value in their homes, and it will be necessary to use the "homestead exemption" that we are discussing here.

This homestead exemption has no effect on your mortgage or any other voluntary lien secured by your home. These "voluntary secured" creditors must be paid or they will be allowed to foreclose. Please remember also that these laws are complex and the benefits provided to debtors depend on some factors and details that are too complex to explain here. Talk to a certified bankruptcy specialist about your situation to be certain of how the laws will affect you and your property!

The Dollar Value of the California Homestead Exemption

California law provides a homestead exemption for $75,000 of equity in your home if you are an individual; or a total of $100,000 if the debtor and spouse reside in the home as a family unit.

The law also protects $175,000 of equity in your home if you are age 65 or older of if you are mentally or physically disabled. If you are over 55, but not yet 65 years old, the larger homestead exemption ($175,000) will also apply to you if your income is under listed amounts ($25,000 or less of gross income for an individual; $35,000 for a married couple).

The larger homestead ($175,000) also applies to you if you are under 65 years of age, but are mentally or physically disabled such that you are unable to engage in substantial gainful employment. The law provides you with a rebuttable presumption that you are "disabled" if you are receiving disability insurance benefit payments under federal social security or under supplemental security income (SSI).

Calculating the Equity in Your Home

The "equity" protected as exempt refers to the value over and above what is owed on the property in mortgages or other voluntary liens.

For example, if your home is worth $400,000 and your mortgage totals $225,000, the "equity" of $175,000 would be protected if you are 65 years old or older. Under these facts, the bankruptcy TRUSTEE would not be allowed to sell your home for the benefit of creditors in your bankruptcy case because the TRUSTEE could not show that a forced sale would result in enough cash to pay the mortgage(s) and to pay you the entire $175,000 plus some additional net cash to pay toward to creditors in the bankruptcy case.

But if the facts are the same ($400,000 home value and $225,000 in mortgage) and you only qualify for the $75,000 homestead available to a single person, then the TRUSTEE could sell your home, pay off the mortgage, give you $75,000 of the net proceeds and keep the balance to give to your creditors.

So you can see that the homestead exemption has limits, and even if you properly claim the exemption, it does not always mean that you will keep your home.

The Homestead Exemption Does Not Affect Your Mortgage

The homestead exemption does not protect you from a mortgage or other "voluntary" lien that you signed for the benefit of a creditor. You will have to make your mortgage payments and the homestead will not stop the lender from eventually foreclosing on your home if you default.

Does the Homestead Exemption Protect Your Mobile Home?

The homestead exemption applies to virtually any type of "dwelling", not just traditional real estate. The definition of a dwelling under California law is broad and includes a mobile home, a boat, a condominium or a stock cooperative, among other things. Of course, you must live in the dwelling for the exemption to apply.

What is a "Homestead Declaration"?

A "homestead declaration" is a legal form that you may record with the County Recorder's office (in the California county where your home is located) and is available as protection before you file a bankruptcy case. It serves as *prima facie evidence* of the facts—that the property is your home and that it is protected by the homestead exemption. Of course, if these "facts" are not true or if the facts have changed since you recorded the declaration, you may have a problem.

The amount of equity protected by a "homestead declaration" is the same as for the homestead exemption described above. If you file bankruptcy, your lawyer will have to properly claim the correct exemptions on the bankruptcy papers filed with the court, regardless of what you may have filed with the County Recorder before bankruptcy.

Should I File a Homestead Declaration Before I File Bankruptcy?

This will be up to you and your attorney to decide. So why would someone file a homestead declaration in California outside of bankruptcy? There are some benefits.

For example, the recorded homestead declaration will protect the cash or other proceeds of a sale of your home if those proceeds are used to buy another home within 6 months and if you also record a homestead declaration on the next home. The normal or "automatic homestead" protection provided by the laws described above *will not* protect these sale proceeds. So, if you might have to sell your home with a judgment creditor lurking out there, anxious to grab escrow proceeds of a sale, this could be an important benefit.

In addition, a recorded homestead declaration may continue to protect the allowed equity amount in your home *after your death for the benefit of certain family members*. This is sometimes referred to as the "probate homestead". If, at the time of your death, the declared homestead is also the principal dwelling of your surviving spouse or another qualified member of your family, your legal exemption will continue to protect the equity in that home from your creditors--provided your surviving spouse or other family member is the successor owner (the person to whom your ownership interest in the home passes at your death). This protection is found in Calif. Code of Civ. Proc., section 704.995.

ABOUT THE AUTHOR
LEON BAYER

A practicing attorney since
1979, Leon Bayer is a founding
partner in the law firm of Bayer
Wishman & Leotta (1989) serving
clients in the Los Angeles,
California area and surrounding
counties. He is a *Certified*

*Specialist in Consumer and Small Business Bankruptcy
Law* by the State Bar of California Board of Legal
Specialization.

With decades of experience, Mr. Bayer and his law firm
provide immediate solutions to people struggling with debts
by using a simple and consistent approach to providing
quality service—every person that contacts their firm for
advice gets a free consultation and an honest assessment of
their legal rights whether or not they decide to hire Bayer
Wishman & Leotta to handle their legal matter.

Mr. Bayer is a highly sought-after speaker, writer and
editor on legal topics including bankruptcy, debt relief, credit,
consumer credit fraud, loan modification scams, foreclosure
rights, the bankruptcy means test, Chapter 13 practice and
procedure, Chapter 7 and avoiding mistakes before and after
filing bankruptcy.

As a consumer rights advocate, Mr. Bayer has many years
of experience writing "tips" and "help" articles as well as
fielding questions from and providing answers to people with
debt, foreclosure and money questions. In addition to his law

firm's blog, Mr. Bayer writes a bankruptcy advice column—
called "ASK LEON"–for the legal publishing powerhouse,
the Nolo Network. You can find Mr. Bayer's advice column
at the Nolo Bankruptcy, Debt & Foreclosure Blog.

Mr. Bayer's latest writing project for legal publisher Nolo
is The New Bankruptcy: Will It Work for You?, 5th Edition,
May 2013.

Mr. Bayer's publications include Best Practices for Filing
Chapter 13: Leading Lawyers on Analyzing Today's Chapter
13 Filings, Preparing Clients, and Implementing Effective
Strategies (Inside the Minds), Thompson Reuters, Aspatore
Books, 2011 ed.; and Trends in Consumer Bankruptcy
Filings: Leading Lawyers on Understanding the Current
Bankruptcy Landscape, Navigating the Filing Process, and
Educating Clients (Inside the Minds), Thompson Reuters,
Aspatore Books, 2010 ed. Other publications are "The
Essentials Of Chapter 13," Daily Journal Report, December
18, 1987; Contributing Editor, Basic Bankruptcy-California
Practice Handbook, Matthew Bender 1992, 1993, and as
Reviewer and Contributor for CEB –Bankruptcy Practice
Guide (2003).

Mr. Bayer has been a frequent law lecturer for numerous
programs, including the semi-annual Bridging the Gap
program for the Los Angles Lawyer's Club and the Daily
Journal Corporation, 1999, 2000, 2001 and 2004, State Bar of
California Annual Meetings, 1984, 1986, 1987, 1988, 1989;
California Bankruptcy Forum, and programs presented by the
United States Trustee. Media appearances include
TELEVISION: KCAL9-Various interviews as Bankruptcy
expert for 2 part series with Reporter Alan Mendelson, How
to Survive the Recession, 3/2002; also Unmasking a Debt
Negotiation Scam, 5/2002; 11/2003, EXTRA - various

interviews as legal expert regarding celebrity bankruptcy cases including Burt Reynolds, Anna Nicole Smith; RADIO: Frequent guest as the bankruptcy expert on the Benjamin Dover Show, KFI; Sunday Edition, public affairs program- 1/03, 97.1 FM, and frequent appearances on Your Legal Rights (2/04) on KALW-FM (91.7), San Francisco, California, KGIL AM.

Mr. Bayer has also been an active member of professional associations related to his practice including the Los Angeles Bankruptcy Forum, the Los Angeles County Bar Association Committee on Commercial Law & Bankruptcy and the Law Advisory Commission-Personal & Small Business Bankruptcy Law of the State Bar of California. From 1995 to 1996, Mr. Bayer served as the President of the Los Angeles Bankruptcy Forum.

ABOUT THE AUTHOR
JEFFREY WISHMAN

A practicing attorney since 1980, Mr. Wishman is a founding partner in the law firm of **Bayer, Wishman & Leotta** (1989) and is a *Certified Specialist in Consumer & Small Business Bankruptcy Law* by the State Bar of California Board of Legal Specialization.

Mr. Wishman adds his degree in accounting to decades of experience as a bankruptcy lawyer helping clients in the Los Angeles and Southern California areas. His easy manner and his command of the nuances of bankruptcy law and the bankruptcy court system combine to immediately put clients' anxieties to rest.

He and his law firm take pride in their honest and consistent approach to providing quality service to people with debt problems—every person that contacts his firm for advice gets a free consultation and an honest assessment of their legal rights whether or not they decide to hire Bayer Wishman & Leotta to handle their legal matter.

In 2003, as recognition for his commitment to pro bono legal work in his community, Mr. Wishman won the *William J. Lasarow Award* presented by the *Public Counsel Law Center.* Public Counsel, the nation's largest pro bono law firm, honors volunteers like Mr. Wishman for donating their time to make access to justice a reality for individuals and families who have nowhere else to turn for legal assistance and representation.

When the news media need experts on bankruptcy law, it's not unusual for Mr. Wishman to get a call and to appear on camera. This was the case in July of 2011 when Fox News LA did a story on the Dodgers then recent Chapter 11 reorganization filing. As a featured television expert, Mr. Wishman correctly predicted that the owners of the franchise would be forced to sell the baseball team in a bankruptcy auction setting.

Mr. Wishman is an active member of professional associations related to his practice including the Los Angeles Bankruptcy Forum and the National Association of Consumer Bankruptcy Attorneys. He also taught bankruptcy law from 1987-1989 as an Instructor at the Santa Monica College Paralegal School.

Mr. Wishman has served as a Contributing Editor to the Legal Assistance, Practice Handbook, Practicing Law Institute, 1986-1991. His lectures, public speaking engagements and related publications include: "Bankruptcy Basics", 2009, a seminar sponsored by the Public Counsel Law Center, Professional Education System's "Bankruptcy Procedures in the Central District of California", 1990; Practicing Law Institute's "Workshop for Legal Assistance in Bankruptcy", 1982-1989 (Los Angeles, San Francisco and Chicago); Community Financial Resource Center's Workshop, "Is Bankruptcy The Solution To Your Debt Problem?", 1995; Matthew Bender's "Emerging Issues In Consumer Bankruptcy", 1997; National Association of Consumer Bankruptcy Attorney's Convention (Law Practice Management), 1997; Los Angeles County Bar Association's "Public Debtor Assistance Program," 1998; The Lawyer's Club of Los Angeles' "Bridging The Gap", 1999-2002, 2005,

2006 and 2009; and the U.S. Trustee program on "Post Confirmation Issues in Chapter 13 Cases", 2002.

* * *

www.ingramcontent.com/pod-product-compliance
Lightning Source LLC
Chambersburg PA
CBHW072025190526
45166CB00015B/497